I0813237

THE NATURE OF PAIN

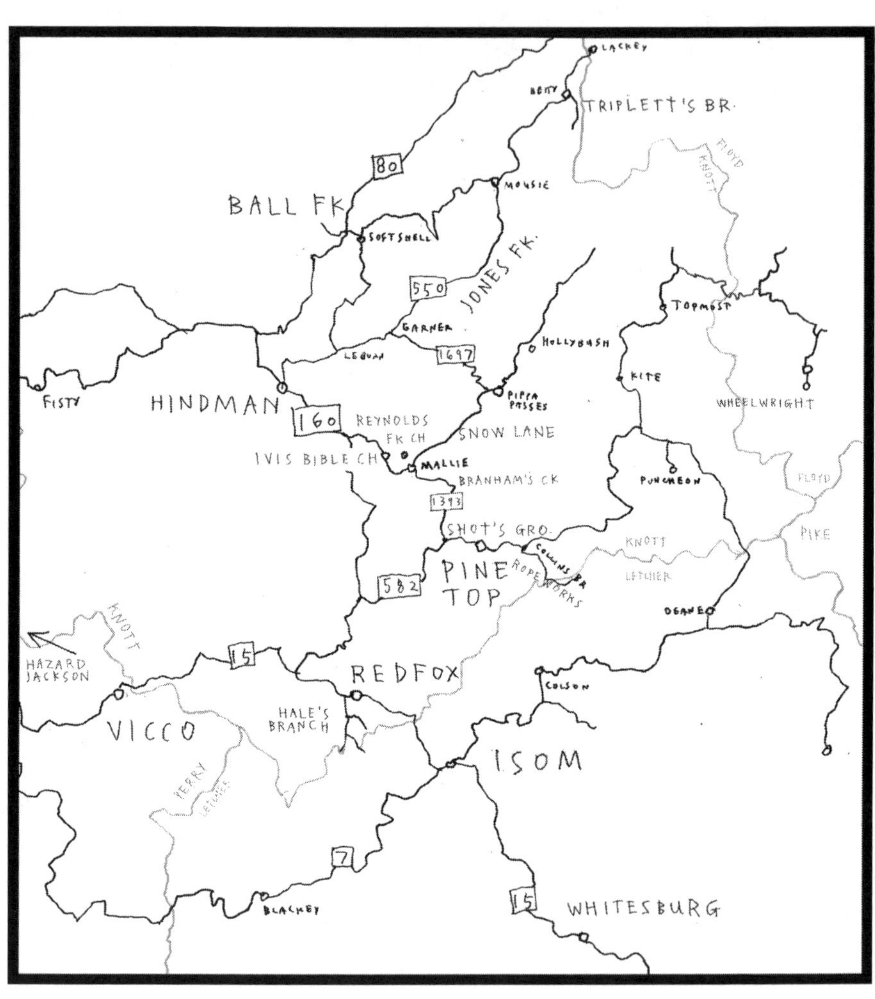

LACKEY
BETTY
TRIPLETT'S BR.
FLOYD
KNOTT
80
BALL FK
MOUSIE
SOFTSHELL
JONES FK.
550
GARNER
LEBURN
1697
HOLLYBUSH
TOPMOST
KITE
WHEELWRIGHT
FISTY
HINDMAN
PIPPA PASSES
160
REYNOLDS FK CH
SNOW LANE
IVIS BIBLE CH
MALLIE
BRANHAM'S CK
1393
PUNCHEON
FLOYD
PIKE
SHOT'S GRO.
KNOTT
COLLINS BR
ROPE WORKS
PINE TOP
LETCHER
582
DEANE
HAZARD
JACKSON
KNOTT
15
REDFOX
COLSON
VICCO
HALE'S BRANCH
ISOM
PERRY
LETCHER
7
BLACKEY
15
WHITESBURG

THE NATURE OF PAIN

ROOTS, RECOVERY, AND REDEMPTION AMID THE OPIOID CRISIS

MANDI FUGATE SHEFFEL

A note to the reader: This volume contains descriptions of drug use, overdose, homicide, and other sensitive topics. Events are portrayed to the best of the author's memory and ability to verify facts. Discretion is advised.

"Grey Goose Chandelier" was originally published in a slightly different form in *Still: The Journal,* issue 37 (Fall 2021).

Published by the University Press of Kentucky,
scholarly publisher for the Commonwealth, serving Bellarmine University, Berea College, Centre College of Kentucky, Eastern Kentucky University, The Filson Historical Society, Georgetown College, Kentucky Historical Society, Kentucky State University, Morehead State University, Murray State University, Northern Kentucky University, Spalding University, Transylvania University, University of Kentucky, University of Louisville, University of Pikeville, and Western Kentucky University.

Editorial and Sales Offices: The University Press of Kentucky
663 South Limestone, Lexington, Kentucky 40508-4008
www.kentuckypress.com

Map by Robert Gipe. Photographs are from the author's collection.

Cataloging-in-Publication data is available from the Library of Congress.

ISBN 978-1-9859-0310-4 (hardcover : alk. paper)
ISBN 978-1-9859-0311-1 (epub)
ISBN 978-1-9859-0312-8 (pdf)

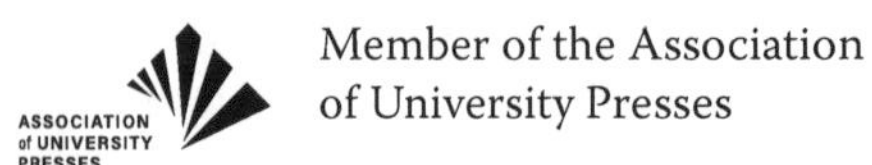

Member of the Association
of University Presses

For Gurney

Eric,

I started writing to you, about you, the week you died, desperately hanging on to what was left of the life we shared. We were family. We were best friends. I had this fear that I would forget you, so I wrote it all down. I wrote in the car, and I wrote at home, and I wrote notes on my phone in the grocery store line. Everywhere I went reminded me of you—thirty years of memories—like an assault on my mind.

I grieved you and what your life could have been. I grieved that you were taken away. I grieved that I had to leave you to save myself when I got clean. Writing helped me process unfinished business—conversations we never had the chance to have.

You live on through me and my work. I'm still here to tell our story. I'm here trying to tell your story—the one cut short. You were robbed of the benefits of aging and hindsight. As time passed, I better understood how and why we became addicted. But we were always more than our addiction. If you were here today, we could laugh about these stories and wonder how we made it through. But you're not here, so I am writing to you, and I am writing for you. The following pages are a testament to who you were, who we were, and who we might have been.

As long as I'm here, I will never let the world forget you.

I love and miss you.

MANDI

Contents

In Remembrance: Tuesday, January 22, 2013 1

Newcomer: 1986–1996

What's in a Name? 7

Hale's Branch 13

Christmas Wish Book 23

Smokin' 29

Fire in the Hole 33

Water 37

Sunday 41

Summertime 45

WBCR 49

Saturday Nights and Sunday Mornings 52

Five Miles 54

Peeling Apples 59

Addiction: 1997–2004

Freedom 65

The Whore from Hardburly 70

Coal Camp Cocaine 73

Ropeworks 79

Pikeville College 85

Johnson City 91

Summer of Fun 97

Euclid Avenue 102

Bust It Up 106

Lethal Combination 110

Acceptance: 2005–2013

Before There Was Treatment 119

Next Step 126

Birthmark 131

Riding in Cars 135

Wednesday, January 16, 2013 139

Thursday, January 17, 2013 141

Friday, January 18, 2013 143

Saturday, January 19, 2013 145

Songs I Wish You Knew: 2013–2020

Uneasy 149

Running Down a Dream 153

Grey Goose Chandelier 157

Epilogue 161

The Last of the Two of Us 164

Acknowledgments 173

About the Author 175

In Remembrance

Tuesday, January 22, 2013

Eric wouldn't have been surprised to see the cast of characters that gathered on the green-carpeted front porch of the Hindman Funeral Home. Coming in and out the front doors, smoking, laughing, hugging, and telling stories. Young and old, friends and family, past and present. Everyone he knew from all walks of life. Heads down, forlorn. I could hear them mumble, "Another one gone too soon."

It seems like death is the only thing that can bring together such an array of people from the same community. I've watched many come and go. My uncle David was first, when he died in 2008 of a heart attack. Then it felt like a domino effect. Three years before Eric, I saw my daddy lying here. Six months before that, my beloved papaw. Ten years later, I'm back in this funeral home with a lot of the same people. People coming to pay their respects as my family laid to rest my aunt Vicki. Four months later, it was Eric's mom—my aunt Jenny. I'm no stranger to the Hindman Funeral Home.

Eric's death was different. At the funeral home, I didn't want to chitchat; I didn't want to be there. How was I supposed to make small talk when my world was falling apart? There was nothing small there. Eric had his whole life ahead of him. Now, as we gathered to celebrate the life that he had, he would never know how much better things could have been—though how could I know for sure that things would have gotten better for him?

Through the double glass doors stood a wooden podium where visitors could sign their names. Beside the large, leather-bound book of signatures were the funeral programs, printed on computer paper and folded in half. I took one to keep. As if I'll ever need this piece of paper to tell me when he was born or when he was gone for good. On the front, the black-and-white headshot that our cousin Amber took right after he got engaged. It wasn't until that night, at that moment at the Hindman Funeral Home, that I looked at his picture and truly saw what he looked like for the first time. He wasn't my coworker, my lover, or my son. He was my best friend from as early as I can remember.

We were connected through blood and hardship. Through childhood innocence and joy. I looked into his eyes, now two-dimensional and Xeroxed, and I could see the spirit I loved. I knew every detail of his face. I knew this face before stubble covered his chin. I knew how his hair would grow long around his ears before he was in control of a standing appointment for a trim. I knew how wrinkles around his eyes were just beginning to show. I knew that face. I know that face.

In the picture, Eric looks handsome and young and seems hopeful for the future. It's black and white, but I looked at his face and could see how it looks like mine—same blue eyes, fair skin, and dirty blond hair. I realized, staring at this funeral bulletin, that I had been seeing Eric the same way for thirty years. I focused on all of those details that day, knowing I would never see that face again.

It feels like everybody in Knott County, Kentucky, has walked this solemn aisle, with green-upholstered benches on each side, murals on the wall of a picturesque valley scene, a box of Kleenex at the end of each row. Pictures and flowers surround the casket, filling the whole room with the smell of a flower shop. Soft-pink recessed light shines on the casket, breaking the room's harsh fluorescents. Above the coffin, a slide show of pictures plays on a drop screen.

Our family worked tirelessly digging out old photos for several days before the funeral. Compiling them was cathartic. We reminisced about good times past. So many stories that flash through my mind like channels changing on a TV. Stories that I felt suddenly afraid I would forget. Stories that will be buried without Eric to retell them with.

In the background, a collection of songs played softly. I had hoped they would brighten the mood yet pay homage to his love of music. The playlist cycles through Hank Jr., Cross Canadian Ragweed, and the Allman Brothers. I couldn't know then, making that playlist, how hard it would be to hear new songs, discover artists, and have no one to share them with. Eric and I had a unity in the soul, and we found that soul in our love for music. Who else would I sit on the phone with for hours dissecting the lyrics of "Stairway to Heaven"? Who would debate with me who was the better guitarist—Stevie Ray Vaughan or Jimi Hendrix? This was our life. We needed music to survive. The quiet and passive nature that we shared made it difficult to communicate our feelings. Music said everything we couldn't.

I was hesitant to approach the casket. I still don't understand the need for this tradition. Others told me I would regret not looking. Later, I would learn that the tradition started with sitting up with the dead back when family members prepared the bodies at home, like the wakes of our European ancestors. Back when it was commonplace for a home to have two front doors, one for family and one for funerals. I learned that two doors made it easier for company to come and go without disrupting the house. Over time, we lost that final connection. What lingers is a sense that we ought to be with the dead somehow. Maybe that's what drives people to want to look inside the casket. I, for one, have never wanted to look. I don't want my last memory to be that one. Eric's siblings, whom he's never met, put a small stuffed bear in the coffin. When he was alive, Eric longed for relationships with them and made up stories about them when we were little. They represented a foundation he needed but never had. Now, there lay the memento of something that was never to be.

One by one, the mourners came to me. I didn't want to talk. I didn't want to discuss what might have happened. I didn't want to be here. The lump in my throat was suffocating. I'm not meant to grieve like this in public, I thought. I wanted to go where I could cry. I wanted to go somewhere without all these eyes. Pain is easier to digest in solitude.

Eric's cousin Randy looked rough. He was the first to approach. His face was pale, his eyes were dark, and his cheekbones were distinguishable. I know this because they dug into my face as he raced to hug me, crying hysterically. He swore he would find out who did this and take care of it. All I wanted was for him to let me go and move on. I was annoyed by his dramatics—more for his benefit than for anyone else. Sitting on the first bench marked family. Mourners came to console me, but there were no words anybody said or could say to change how I felt, to take this pain away, or to put things back together the way they were. What was said didn't matter.

I didn't care who was there. The person I needed was gone—the only person in my life who saw me. Eric and I were both raised in single-parent homes with lots of love. But we were also both very alone—except for one another. We were always more like brother and sister than cousins. Born to young mothers who still had their own growing up to do. Born to absent fathers.

Eric had always been there, regardless of what I did or said. Eric was the only person who listened to me. Eric was the only person I listened to. We did this life together. And suddenly, he was gone. I was left trying to figure out how to navigate the world alone. I had the support and love from the family I made—a husband and a child of my own—but with Eric gone, I felt emotionally isolated. No pain exceeded what I experienced when Eric died. No one could help. I needed to grieve alone.

NEWCOMER
1986–1996

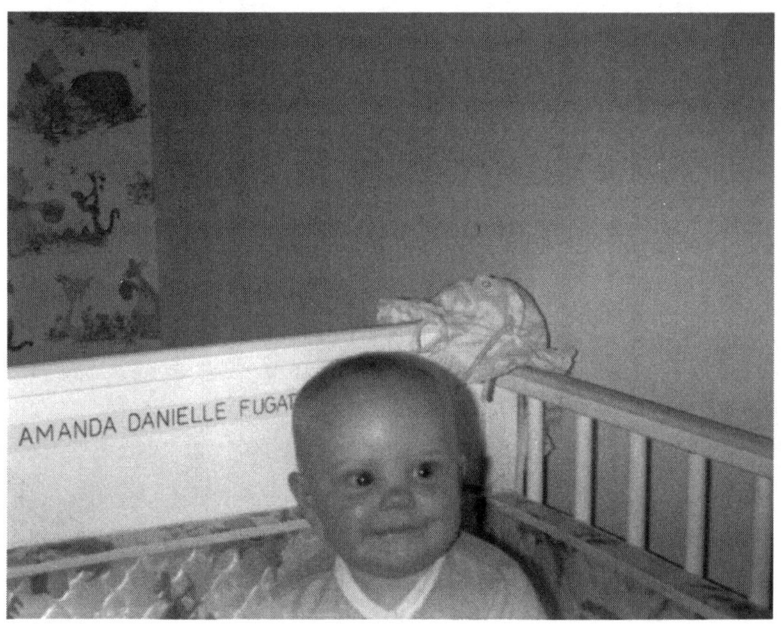

Mandi, seven months

What's in a Name?

My parents named me after a country music outlaw. My daddy loved Waylon Jennings. It seemed fitting that his only daughter carry the name of one of Waylon's most iconic ballads. Originally released by Don Williams, "Amanda" became a hit for Waylon in 1974. By the time I was born in 1981, this song was embedded deep into my daddy. We'd listen to Waylon most every weekend, but I never once heard my daddy listen to "Amanda."

My mom still sings "Amanda, light of my life" anytime she can work it in. My daddy never sang to me. My mom considered naming me after my dad. Had things turned out differently, I'd be answering to Terry. It might have been Terri with an *i,* like how my mom spelled Mandi. I try to imagine what my life would have been had I been Terry Fugate, the same as my father. I looked like him, moved my hands like him, and liked to drink beer like him. It would have been hard to survive in the shadows of his name.

Eric probably longed for a dad to be named after. My dad became more of a presence in Eric's life than he was in mine. Because Eric was a boy, there were things my dad thought he needed, skill sets that someone needs to teach a boy. How to mow the grass. How to change the oil. How to bait a hook. Eric's dad was never around, so my dad became that someone.

I've spent my whole life clarifying the spelling of my nickname. Amanda Danielle Fugate, my full name at birth—Amanda, thanks to Waylon, and Danielle for every woman's love of Danielle Steel in the early eighties—but Mandi to everyone who knew me.

I was Amanda during roll call and doctor's appointments. Past that, I didn't associate with that name. I was thirty-two when I got married, and I couldn't let go of Fugate, not on paper or from my bones. In eastern Kentucky, everything we do is tied to our last name. You know someone's whole history just by knowing who their people are. A person's last name gives them a level of creditability in the mountains. It's an immediate source of common ground. Whether good or bad, it's a history rooted in place. My husband's family moved into the region in the early 1950s. The Sheffel name is uncommon. So, I dropped Danielle and became Amanda Fugate Sheffel. I wonder if that hurt my mom's feelings. What's it like for your child to abandon a name you adoringly chose for them? I didn't care. I needed a connection to my past—not the past of my husband's family. I wanted to stay rooted in place with the stories that I grew up with—stories that only existed among the storytellers of my family.

My great-grandpa General Fugate was a story larger than life, with his time as sheriff of Knott County and owner of a local grocery store. Or my grandpa Phil Fugate's drunken car crash that left behind four small children and a widow. These are examples of what people will know about me when they figure out what set of Fugates I'm from. These are the things about my past I don't have to explain when I'm meeting someone near home for the first time. This is part of the comfort for me. Not everyone with the same last name is directly related. It may be that they live in another part of the county or a different community. In that case, they'd be from another set.

Sometimes when I hear people call my name, it sounds weird in their mouths. Almost like my name wasn't meant for others to say. It's a strange sensation. My husband rarely says my name. It's usually "honey," or just "hey." When he does, it draws me to attention. It became a signal that something is wrong. It's not something we decided; it's one of those unspoken things that develops over time. My dad called me Danielle or Fart, never Mandi. He always called Eric E.T. because his middle name was Tysen. He gave everyone a nickname. His sister Jennifer became Fur, and, to my daddy, his friends were Hollywood, Wormy, and

Bubba. Sometimes he'd refer to my mom, Charlotte, as Red because of her long red hair. He didn't say her name much; he'd usually just call her my mother.

Eric just called me Mandi.

Eric and I were both comfortable going unnoticed. I've always felt like I have a mouth full of marbles when I introduce myself. I wondered if Eric felt that way. I know he dreaded introductions too. Mandi never comes out clean and strong. What always follows is "Brandi?" or "Andi?" I wished for a name no one would confuse. I wished for a name that didn't cause my face to turn red in anticipation of clarification. And maybe none of this would have mattered for a kid who wasn't so painfully shy. I wanted nothing more than to disappear. All my name ever did was make interactions challenging. Make me stand out. I let teachers call me Amanda even though no one else did because I couldn't speak up in front of the class to tell them I'd prefer Mandi. I let people call me Andi because I could never correct anyone.

I didn't get my mom's red hair or my dad's brown eyes. I didn't get their ability to command a room. But I stand like my dad: butt out, pinkie out, one hand on my hip, the other motioning as I speak. I have strong opinions and the ability to survive like my mother. She was never afraid to stand up for what she believed in, and her beliefs spilled out for everyone around her to absorb. She was raised Jehovah's Witness and was never allowed to date or listen to secular music. There were no holidays, birthdays, or school dances in her world. This made her a target for teasing and ridicule among people her age. Her mother also battled an untreated mental illness. She wasn't very attentive to my mom or her sister, so they were responsible for getting themselves up and ready for school at an early age. Mom often went to school smelling bad and wearing dirty clothes. This, coupled with a strange religion, made my mom's early childhood a nightmare. My grandmother told her kids she wished they were never born. My mom made sure she told me how much she loved and wanted me every day. She was a child who had a child.

I grew up on government assistance and free preschool. My mom was alone and had to make a life for us somehow. She was putting herself through school all while raising me. She taught me about perseverance and the realities of being on your own. Early on, it was expected that I learn to be independent. She knew how important being able to take care of yourself was. My affinity for escape could have come from anywhere. My dad was always searching for that escape. There was always somewhere better than where he was.

My dad listened to Bob Seger's "Travelin' Man" to keep his search for escape going. He never told me that. I just imagined that the lyrics said all the things he never did. I picture him behind the wheel of his old Jeep truck, windows down, cigarette between his fingers, the wind swirling through the cab. When I was young, sitting in the passenger seat, I liked the driving bass line and the tempo change of the song. It conjured emotions in me that made me feel like we could conquer the world. It wouldn't be until much later that I realized these lyrics epitomize my dad's lived experience.

If ever a film was made about my dad, this would be the song that played over all his failed attempts at settling down. The only version he would listen to was on *Live Bullet*—the double live album from Detroit 1975. "Travelin' Man" flows seamlessly into "Beautiful Loser," and I couldn't think of a more perfect pairing. This feeling of needing to escape is prevalent in my life as it was in his, and his father's before him. This was never anything we talked about; it was just something we did. He did.

DNA is funny like that. It makes it hard to sort out what was bound to happen and what you pick up along the way. Is trauma passed down from generation to generation? What about a sense of humor? Or ease of temperament? What about addiction?

Eric and I were alike in a lot of ways. He was passive, like me. He became addicted, like me. He bottled up his feelings and feared letting anyone get close. He kept quiet unless he was sure about what he had to say. He never commanded attention. He was content in his own company with an element of discomfort when there was someone else to tend to. All of that felt familiar to me. Were these traits genetic or environmental?

Addiction is an anomaly to people who have healthy coping skills. For most of the population, it's hard to understand the need to gravitate toward things that have a negative impact on their lives. It's slippery and difficult to categorize. I know that once something changes the way I feel, I want more of whatever that is—ritualized, compulsive comfort-seeking. It's been alcohol and drugs, sugar, travel, and love—specifically, it's been alcohol and drugs. Drugs were consistent and dependable. When I had drugs, I didn't need anybody else. The social skills I lacked didn't matter. Everything I feared disappeared. The inability to make connections was gone. The fear of abandonment was gone. The sense that nobody would ever understand me was gone. This is what I tried to escape. This is what I sought.

I guess it was the same for Eric. All of that works until it doesn't, until you're left with that deep-seated loneliness. My mom's words play repeatedly in my head, "No matter where you go, there you are." There truly is no way to escape your mind. Addiction is a symptom of something deeper. Habits are cyclic. Habits are ingrained in our very makeup. Long after I took that last drink, I wanted more. I still feel like an appendage has been removed. There is a hole. There is pain.

I work hard to break the cycle. I want it for me, but I also want it for my son. I want a new way of life for us all. But no matter how much I want to change, some things inevitably stay the same. The depression and anxiety I can see so clearly now, in my past and present, are overwhelming and motivating. Yet, these things are hidden, buried, tucked away, waiting like constant reminders.

I was named after a country music outlaw and his vision of a woman. I was named after an idea that probably could never really be. I wonder how much that start—that first seed of who I would be—shaped who I could become. I wonder what was laid out for Eric and me by the parents who weren't ready for us. How did "Travelin' Man" and "Beautiful Loser" map a route for us both, and why did I find my way onto a different path when so many people around me couldn't?

Mandi and Papaw Bill, 1984

Hale's Branch

God's country is what my papaw called it. Hills where wild teaberry grows, whole flats of it in the underbrush on the mountain behind his house. Papaw showed me how to identify it, and we'd chew it like gum. The creeks were as clear and cold as nature would allow. I hung on his every word like it was gold. It was just a few acres of land in the head of a holler in eastern Kentucky. It wasn't a sprawling bluegrass horse farm; there were no barns or bourbon barrels. No caverns carved out of limestone. And it most definitely wasn't a bustling metropolis. It was the forgotten part of Kentucky, coal country. Everything east of I-75 and south of I-64. But to him, it was a piece of heaven. He couldn't fathom the thought of ever leaving.

I wonder if Eric thought about leaving. It was a conversation we never had the chance to have. I always imagined my life with some connection to Hale's Branch. I knew I'd go away to school, but when I imagined my life after that, it was here in eastern Kentucky. Maybe Eric didn't feel that same connection, without the tie to generations of family land. In Hale's Branch, I had a landing spot, a place I knew I could always come home to. The Fugates didn't have that family history on one plot of land.

My papaw only left once, to go to war. He joined the navy and was stationed off the coast of Florida. He never saw any action . . . unless you count booze and women. He promptly returned when his time was up. He was the fifth generation of Hales to spend his days in this holler. I am the seventh.

I spent my days wandering the hillsides and playing in the creek. Sometimes I went to the old abandoned mine where water sees first light, where generations before me dug coal on their hands and knees to provide the warmth they would so badly need come winter. All the water we drank came from black pipes shoved in the hillside, gravity-fed to our houses. This water made its way through layers of shale and limestone, trickling through the mountain and running deep underground. I am this mountain, and this water is me.

Hale's Branch is the safest place I have ever known. It was my papaw Bill that made it feel this way. One hundred and fifty years of Hales, my ancestors, calling this valley home. The hollow is narrow—hillside, creek, road, and then hillside. Just enough room to carve out a house seat. It's lush and beautiful in the summer. The creek is cool and gives relief from the sweltering Kentucky heat. Then there's fall, with all its orange and red, cool nights, and the comfort of a warm bed. Winter is sparse and gray and makes the roadway hard to navigate. Springtime is fragrant with wildflowers and the return of wildlife. When I smell honeysuckle, I am at Hale's Branch with Eric. I remember all the times we stopped to suck on the blooms.

My papaw never missed a chance to work in a story, like the one about how his Granny Hale promised all her sons $500 if they waited until they were thirty to get married because she believed marriage enslaved men. They were educators and some of the first college graduates in the area. His Pa Hale read the paper to everyone around the store on Sunday mornings. Papaw liked to tell stories about his uncles who lived there before us. His uncles were all athletes, often competing to divvy up the chores. They would shoot at cans or play tennis in the yard that they had turned into a court. I took after them as a tennis player. Another favorite pastime was drinking and playing cards. Papaw would tell about when he won the property at the mouth of the holler in a card game, or how he won a diamond ring his Pa Hale gave his grandma on their fiftieth wedding anniversary. Or how he rotted out the seat of his '57 Chevy from the beer can he kept between his legs. I took after him as a drinker.

I knew there were hard times, too. Subjects that don't make for entertaining stories. Like his uncle Oscar's death by suicide or his aunt Ellie's shock treatments. How his cousin Archie died at the kitchen table after a night of drinking. That same night, he'd sworn off drinking forever. The types of stories you hear when you're not supposed to be listening. Information that I don't remember acquiring.

These were just stories with Papaw. When I was with my dad, though, I lived things I shouldn't have, and that was the difference. Carrying around family history from hearsay and living it are two different things. I should have never seen all the drinking and drug use. Maybe that added to my anxiety. I didn't have to worry about people from the past, whom I only heard about in stories. I did have to worry about my dad and my mom. I worried about what would happen if I wasn't there to protect them. My papaw's stories gave me a better understanding of where I came from. I understood why his uncles loved this place. I understood why Papaw loved this place. I started to understand why I loved this place. I was a part of something bigger. Eric was missing that generational connection to a piece of land. I wonder if he thought about that.

My parents married in Clintwood, Virginia, on January 19, 1980. My mom says everybody got married in Clintwood around that time. If you went to Virginia, you could skip the three-day waiting period and get married that same day. Seems to me that maybe they needed a few more days to think. They came home to Hale's Branch, my great-great-grandparents' cabin built in the late 1800s. Hand-hewed logs, two rooms, one on top of another, and no bathroom or running water. They came home to a new television set, a cake, and a bottle of champagne. She was nineteen. He was twenty-six. My mother dreamed of a life as a homemaker. My dad dreamed of a life with no boundaries or responsibilities. The following day, after finishing the champagne, he decided it was time to go. My dad let my mom know her place was at home, not as his running mate. She knew she had made a mistake.

They divorced on April 1, 1982. It makes me wonder why or how they ever thought a marriage would work. I think my mom was smitten by my dad's worldly ways, long curly hair, and brown eyes. When she turned eighteen and left the church, a whole new world opened up for her. My dad was there to usher her in. Only seven years her senior, he had already lived the life of most grown folks, well into alcohol and drugs and a life of freedom she knew nothing about. It must have looked exotic to her—his carefree attitude and take-it-as-it-comes point of view. He gave her attention and took interest in her—something she longed for.

She needed someone to see her, desire her, and love her. Maybe she thought her love was enough to make him settle down to live the traditional married life she'd only read about in books. Then came me. I know my mom wanted a baby girl. She has told me so my whole life: how she threw her birth control pills down the hole in the outhouse and wanted nothing more than to be a mother. Having me also feels like an attempt to complete that fantasy she created. Maybe she thought I would also help guide him into a life of domestication. Neither of those things worked. There was something in her that needed to feel loved and needed. There was something in him that needed to feel free and untethered.

He never denied me. He couldn't really. My mom was a virgin before she met my dad. She says I was conceived to "Free Bird"—so that basically ruined "Free Bird" for me. I don't know if that's true or if it's one of those things that adds to a story's value as you tell it through the years. Regardless, I've never liked that song.

She wanted so badly to have something different than the home she was raised in that she couldn't see the pitfalls that would come with trying to make that home with my dad. He taught her the meaning of love *and* loss. She let my dad go once she got what she wanted—a child. He was determined to not be contained by anyone or anything. And he wasn't, right up until the day he died, precisely twenty-eight years to the day after they got divorced. He died untethered, and she never married again. I think she's still searching for that something to make her feel whole. I think he must have been searching for something else.

When my mom lost her focus and my dad went on to carve his path, my papaw was my one constant, just like our Granny B was Eric's constant. After my parent's divorce, my mom and I moved in with Papaw down the road in Hale's Branch. He was recently divorced and probably thinking he would lead the life of a bachelor when we came along. He took us in. He had a quick wit and a love of basketball, which he passed on to me. He was never affectionate, always telling me cowboys don't hug. But I knew he loved me and would make sure I was taken care of, no matter what happened. He was the reason Hale's Branch was a safe place. He filled in all the places my dad could only be in on the weekends. He was sober and dependable. Tight as bark on a tree, he made sure I knew how wasteful my parents were and what I needed to do to not be a "broke ass" like them.

My papaw chewed Levi Garrett chewing tobacco and spat in a peach can. I can see the brown package creased from being folded over and over, the lettering looking like something from a Western. The peach can with the label peeling off, its perfect wide mouth for spitting. He loved canned peaches and would eat one of those big cans himself. When he was a boy, growing up in the Depression, peaches were a treat he rarely enjoyed. His mother raised him and his siblings alone. His father died of tuberculosis when he was eighteen months old. He told me these stories. Tobacco spit would run down the corners of his mouth.

My papaw's place was a haven of stock market recaps, Kentucky basketball games, and Chef Boyardee. I'm almost positive that man never ate a can of ravioli in his life, but it was there when I needed it. His house always smelled like tobacco juice and Old Spice. The TV was turned up loud, and he never adjusted the volume. We all just talked louder. Papaw and I watched Kentucky basketball games together, but he always preferred listening to Cawood Ledford call the games, and this was the only time he would turn down the TV to turn on the radio.

Papaw played basketball at Carr Creek High School, and that, by his account, was his greatest achievement. I decided I wanted basketball to be my greatest achievement. I stopped playing basketball in eighth grade. I was only good in my yard when nobody was watching. Seems like I was always better at things when people weren't watching.

Those days at Carr Creek superseded his time in the navy and his children. He retired from the railroad with a hearing injury in 1982, when I was a year old, and I never saw him work a day. He reminisced about his days as an engineer, how he would toot the horn when he came back into the yards—two shorts and a long on the whistle to let his wife know to put supper on. He taught me how to shoot foul shots. He taught me how to fry cabbage. He taught me how to take care of myself. In his world, there were no "man jobs." You did what you had to do to take care of things.

Papaw stood in for my father, who was otherwise occupied. He was reliable and did things on a schedule. We mowed grass every Thursday after school whether it needed it or not. He walked the holler every morning and every evening, never growing tired of the same landscape. He liked to court on Wednesday evenings. He had a girlfriend he visited who lived in town. His dependability comforted me in what felt like an otherwise unpredictable existence.

Even though most of my time was spent in Hale's Branch, the stories that press on me are weekends with my dad and Eric. Those are the ones that shaped me. It's not my mom, who went on to get a teaching degree, or my papaw, who taught me to value where I was from. My dad and his freedom and reckless abandon appealed to me the most when I was a kid.

As an only child of a young, single mother in the eighties, I spent a lot of time alone. For me, there's comfort in time spent in solitude: no expectations, no awkward silences, no forced conversations. But there's a difference between being alone and being lonely. My childhood was littered with loneliness. Bits of time when I needed someone to share with. Sometimes that took the form of Christopher Robin, my imaginary friend, around the age of three. One time, we left Christopher Robin at Kmart—something I failed to realize until we were almost home, and I was shouting from the back seat, "We left Christopher Robin." My mom made the drive back to Kmart to pick him up.

Most days, I just talked to myself. I learned to be my favorite company. My mom was young and had a thriving social life outside of me. While I was in good hands in her absence, it wasn't like being at home with my mom in my room. There were times when I longed for that. That I longed for her.

I have never been short on deep feelings. Even from an early age, I felt things on a deeper level. So, with my deep feelings and a flare for the dramatic, I caught my tears in a jar after my mom left for a weekend away. I wasn't crying for her as much as I was crying for something consistent. My space, my time alone, the comfort of being home, couldn't be replicated with my dad, my papaw, or a babysitter. So, I caught my tears in a jar, thinking I could plead my case. This jar of tears was tangible evidence of the pain those weekends away inflicted on me. My ten-year-old mind failed to realize that tears are mostly water and salt and evaporate quickly. All my pain and anguish disappeared into the atmosphere before I could languish. I had nothing to show for all I had felt.

At the time, I knew nothing about tear jars that have existed for thousands of years. They were used by mourners in ancient societies to collect tears and bury them with loved ones or mark the time of grief. When the tears evaporated, the grieving period was over. But my mom wasn't dead, and I wasn't grieving. I was a sad kid who gave way to a sad adolescent and bled into a sad adult. That lingering feeling just at the bottom of my throat, in the center of my chest, waiting to build, longing to bust open and flood everything.

But I didn't let those feelings show. Even if my tears hadn't evaporated, I wouldn't have shown them to my mom. Tear catching was for me only. My emotions were mine alone. Around my friends and at school, I was considered a class clown and a gross overachiever. People wouldn't see the real me if I could be smart enough and funny enough. That worked for a long time. That worked for most of my life. Even when I was using, I maintained that control. I was easy and responsible. No one noticed I was spiraling out of control. I could spend my morning at the National Honor Society induction and the evening smoking pot and snorting coke.

I went to great lengths to avoid feeling like I didn't belong. There was something about me that was different from my friends. In my advanced placement classes, I felt alone, yet I was a nerd to everyone I partied with. So, I stayed on the periphery of every social function I attended. But I learned quickly that when I was high, I didn't care; I could tap into that comfort of solitude from when I was a kid. If I don't let them in, they can't hurt me.

I learned early that place was more important than people—place was something I could trust. Place was dependable. In my early experience, people came with disappointment and were prone to acting on whims. I was born to young parents, and they had their own growing up to do. That left me mature beyond my years, with a need to be responsible for myself and those around me. I wanted to ease the burden for them. I never wanted to be needy. I lived to make them laugh, to take our situation and make it something more livable. I learned the power of a good one-liner.

I buried my feelings and knew that I could always depend on myself. My temperament was easy, but my insides were churning. I wanted people to stay, and to make them stay, I became someone who lost her voice. I'd like to say that somewhere along the way I found that voice, but I'm not sure that's true. I still want to make people laugh. I still fear being needy or becoming a burden to those I depend on. I never want to take up too much space in any situation I find myself in. It's easier now, but even in the spaces I've been able to assert myself, there's still a little voice inside telling me to keep quiet and step out of the light. When my circle of people becomes too large, I want to retreat to the comfort of solitude. And then the loneliness creeps back in. It's a constant battle with my own mind.

The way I felt at Hale's Branch, with Papaw and basketball on the radio, is a feeling I wouldn't have again. I found all sorts of ways to chase it, and it made me wonder if it was ever real to begin with.

Mandi and Mom, Christmas 1985

Christmas Wish Book

1986

My parents divorced before my second birthday. I never longed for a family in the traditional sense because I never had one. Being raised by a single mom was something Eric and I had in common. Daddy moved to Florida when I was four. Before the age of ten, that relationship consisted of long-distance phone calls and outlandish gift requests. It seemed like I could ask him for anything, and the package would be on my doorstep in a matter of weeks. I wanted a leather jacket and *Goats Head Soup* by the Rolling Stones. I wanted a leather jacket like Michael Jackson's, but he sent me a black leather Harley-Davidson one with a silver belt at the bottom. He got the Rolling Stones right though. I gave the jacket Daddy sent, which was the wrong jacket, to Eric.

When I saw my dad, it was usually at Christmas, when he, my stepmom, and my two stepbrothers journeyed back to eastern Kentucky to see me. One summer, my dad and stepmom drove up to Kentucky to visit family, pick me up, and return to Florida. I was six, and I was leaving everything I knew for a trip to the beach with people who were essentially strangers to me. Hindman, Kentucky, to Orlando, Florida, is about a twelve-hour drive. Twelve hours in a car with something like strangers is hell when you're six.

I don't remember much of that drive until we T-boned a car in a four-way stop. The driver of the other car was high and had a car full of cocaine. At least that's the way my dad always told it. He never saw us or the stop sign coming. I was sitting in the back seat of a burnt-red Oldsmobile Cutlass, sandwiched between my stepbrothers. That's probably what kept me from flying through the windshield. No one wore seatbelts then. My dad and stepmom both left their head prints in the glass.

The next thing I remembered, I was in the back seat of a police cruiser, and I couldn't get out. All around me, I saw fire trucks and ambulances. I pushed my face into the window, hoping someone would see me, see that I was alone. I wondered where my family was and if I would see them again. Would they remember me? I was scared. Among the lights and the noise and all the people rushing around, it seemed as though I'd been forgotten in the back of this cruiser. When a cop finally noticed me, I had been crying. My memories are blurry, but I had probably peed my pants. That's a detail I don't remember. What I do remember is being escorted to sit with my stepbrother in the back of an ambulance. His face was covered in burns from the cloth upholstery that he had slammed against on impact. In my next memory, we were in the hospital waiting room. My aunt Kat was there, and she was letting me call my mom from a pay phone. She told me everything would be okay. Then I remember puking in a tan, kidney-shaped bowl.

Sometimes I confuse my memory with what I've seen in pictures. My mom, unlike my dad, was diligent with her photo albums. My childhood chronicled month by month, year by year, for the entirety of my life. But there are no pictures of this accident. I finished out that summer sleeping with my stepbrothers on a pallet on the living room floor of my dad's one-bedroom apartment. We still went to Disney and Sea World—my dad with a white bandage and my stepmom in a neck brace. Like most of my childhood injuries, mine weren't visible.

The Christmas when I was five, all of our family gathered at Granny B's house. If my dad was in town, I would spend Christmas Eve with the Fugates at Granny B's, but I was always home, in Hale's Branch, on Christmas morning for Santa. Christmas at Granny B's was my favorite time of year because everyone was there. All six kids. My dad, his two brothers, and three sisters. Then there were the four cousins. Me in the middle, surrounded by Eric and Chase, the younger cousins, and Amber and Shannon, the older cousins. It was different from being at home, where it was just my mom and me. It was vibrant. Everybody battling to tell a story, all the scents coming out of the kitchen—the savory smells of green beans and cornbread and the sweetness of homemade candy.

Granny B always made cornbread in that cast-iron skillet, molded to look like ears of corn. Years later, I learned that my Granny B wasn't a great cook and that, more than likely, anything prepared on Christmas was prepared by my aunt Jenny. I figured this out when Granny B tried to pass off Luck's canned pinto beans as homemade. I've been a soup bean connoisseur my whole life, and I knew a Luck's bean when I tasted one. I never trusted her cooking after that. She wasn't one of those sweet little grannies in the kitchen. She liked to eat, but she'd sure let someone else prepare it. While all this was going on in the kitchen, my dad would hold court with tales about his time working in Florida. He was on a crew that helped build Universal Studios, and his claim to fame was that his initials were carved into the concrete sidewalk.

We knew Christmas was getting close when the Sears Wish Book catalog came in the mail. Granny B would give us kids the Wish Book and tell us to initial anything we might want. We spent hours poring over that catalog. It felt like anything your heart desired could be found on those pages.

Then there was the big screen TV Eric and I always got in trouble for messing with. We couldn't keep our hands off that projection box in the front with the three lights inside: red, blue, and green. Eric was used to being at Granny B's, so I don't think he was as impressed as I was. All he wanted to do was run in and out the back door or up and down the basement stairs, but he followed my lead. To me, those lights were a thing of beauty. I just couldn't control myself. I knew that touching that TV would get us in trouble, but the thrill was worth the risk.

Compared to the black-and-white TV in my room—an old tube TV—this projector was fascinating. In my mind, it made my grandma rich.

When it came time to open gifts, we'd all sit in a circle in the middle of the floor. My grandma watched as one by one we opened gifts. She'd never let us tear into anything unless everyone was watching. Not even the adults.

I always hated this part. I was uncomfortable when my turn came around and everyone was watching. I was worried that my reaction wouldn't be enough or that she'd think I didn't appreciate what was given to me. I was worried that they might think my mom had spoiled me, and Christmas at Granny B's wasn't good enough. I was always grateful for whatever I received, but I never wanted my turn to linger on too long. One Christmas, she gave me a ruffled purple umbrella and Exclamation perfume. I had been disappointed, not so much about the gift but because I felt like she didn't even know me. There was no room for ruffles on the basketball court. But this Christmas, the year I was five, my dad had bought me a Bigfoot Power Wheels. There was no mistaking how much I loved that. Eric and I took turns all day, up and down the driveway at my grandma's house.

Later that night, my mom came to get me so I could have Christmas morning at Hale's Branch. She had been to a Christmas party and had been drinking. I remember the rest of the night in images, like flipping through old photos. No one wanted to let me leave with her. My dad was yelling. My mom was wearing a blue-sequined sweater and a black leather miniskirt. In his jeans and cowboy boots, my uncle David kicked at my mom's car as she pulled away down the gravel drive, making contact with her taillight. Red plastic exploded into pieces and fell to the road. My mom's taillight burned white, blinding when she turned the curve. I stood on the road where I had been driving my new Bigfoot Power Wheels earlier. I wondered how I'd get my Power Wheels home. My dad didn't drive me for the same reason no one wanted me to ride with her. My aunt

Vicki drove me, but no one seemed to mind that. We went from Hindman to Red Fox. I sat up front in my dad's lap as they took me home.

My Bigfoot Power Wheels was still at Granny B's as I fell asleep on the bed I shared with my mom, whose blue-sequined sweater was now covered in vomit.

Mandi and Dad, December 1984

Smokin'

1992

The smell of a Zippo lighter and the smell of liquor. Those are the smells of my daddy. I'm not sure Daddy knew how to entertain me after he moved back to Kentucky. My memories of weekends with him are actually memories of weekends with my aunt Jenny and Granny B. My relationship with him never progressed past awkward and silent. I always felt like there was some barrier I couldn't break through. The wants and needs of a child didn't carry much weight in the world of adult problems, so I learned to build my own wall. Seems like Eric did, too. Could it be that we were born with that wall? I learned that some things are better left unsaid and that finding someone to listen to me felt like an uphill task.

The relationship with my dad might have been doomed from the start. We were too much alike. He was quiet and contemplative and used humor to mask any real issue. Nature or nurture, I became the same. I stayed in the background. I became one of the guys, hanging out with people and places most would consider inappropriate for children. Eric and I hung back, unnoticed, most of these times. There was always that point when Daddy had too much to drink and wanted to talk. His rough, calloused hands held mine as he cried about memories and relationships long gone. He'd cry for me and my half brother, whom he never had a relationship with. I think that haunted him. He mourned not being the parent he should have been to me, though he couldn't express it. He grieved the death of my grandfather, whom he lost when he was seven. He would take me and Eric by the hand and tell us how much he loved us. When he squeezed, I could feel his pain and the deep desire to make us understand, even though he didn't have the words to say it. This was the side of him no one else saw.

Daddy came and went, was expressive or was silent, was laughing or was crying. But there was always Eric, the son of Daddy's youngest sister. We were born one year, three months, and fourteen days apart. We'd be up before dawn, before the fog lifted, dew still on the ground, the air still thick with haze, long before anyone else stirred in the house. The only sound came from a small under-the-counter radio that constantly played the local station, just enough to drown out the loud silence. The place creaked and groaned, but we knew no one would be awake to check on us. Up early, we would find Granny B's cigarette case. I still know just how we eased it open, careful not to be too loud with the snap-on top. Virginia Slims. I can still see the pastel pack with those treasures inside—long, thin, and much too elegant to be cool. I'd only slip one out of the pack because two would get us busted.

We'd head up the hill behind Granny B's house, Eric in his long jean shorts and flea-market Bart Simpson tee and beat-up Converse shoes from a long school year. The gravel driveway we had trekked so many times led to our uncle David's. The same gravel driveway we'd sled down in the winter. The same gravel driveway where we'd learn to drive a car. We explored every inch of that land—the house and the woods, which were, like Uncle David, all products of Granny B's second marriage. Most of the time spent with my dad would be at my grandma's, sneaking off to smoke Virginia Slims and find mischief.

Eric never met his dad, so my dad and David stepped into that role. Eric was definitely Granny B's favorite. She'd always have bologna sandwiches and Mountain Dew for us—but mostly for Eric. We'd find candy bars stashed away everywhere. You know, in case her sugar dropped. We'd sprawl out on her bed and watch MTV eating diabetic candy bars, waiting for Kris

Kross and Nirvana videos. Out on our pretend motorcycles, our mouths making motor sounds, hands stretched out, holding onto handlebars, popping out the kickstand to enjoy a smoke.

Eric would say, "Mom says she's going to buy me Harley Jack's old dirt bike off Ruby when she gets her tax return."

And I'd say, "Yeah? That'll be cool." Because I wanted that to happen for him, but I wasn't sure it would. It seems like when tax time rolled around, something breaking was always more important than a dirt bike.

We would quote lines from *In Living Color*, and he had the perfect Fire Marshal Bill impression. He'd dry off his lips and then fold them under, exposing his teeth. I knew he longed for a dirt bike. I didn't much care, but for now, bicycles would have to do. Remembering this now tells me we were much too young to be partaking in the joys of a Virginia Slim if we were still sneaking candy and dreaming of bicycles.

I can still hear our preteen protest, "I will never smoke! Those things choke me to death. Oh my God, everything smells like stale smoke!" Daddy smoked Vantage. The blue-and-red bull's eye was prominent in the cellophane pack, and I can still remember how it felt to stick my tongue in the little hole at the end of the filter. Daddy used a Zippo. Sometimes I smell it even when no lighter fluid is near, and it makes me feel happy and excited but also anxious about what adventure is around the corner. I have always heard the sense of smell is the one that is most connected to memory. The mixture of lighter fluid and Early Times whiskey carries too much emotion and too many memories.

I wonder what Eric thought when he smelled a Zippo—after he was grown and before he died. I never asked. These are the types of memories and conversations that come with age. Conversations that we would never have. I know Uncle David left Eric his Zippo collection when he died. I always wondered if he kept them as a collection or used any of them. A bunch of old lighters probably doesn't seem like that big of a deal, but our family wasn't one of great wealth, so the smallest of tokens feel like treasures.

It's unbelievable how we both became smokers as much as we hated those things growing up. But there's something about the ritual, the ease with which Daddy pulled a Vantage out of his shirt pocket, smacked it on his palm to pack the tobacco, and with a quick flip, closed the Zippo. I guess we ended up doing a lot of things we said we'd never do. I always felt like I could somehow control it, or that I was smarter than or different from them. Turns out I was wrong.

Fire in the Hole

1992

I don't think anyone would have used the word "bad" to describe Eric and me. We weren't destructive or malicious. We were good to each other, and we mostly respected authority. We were responsible and made some good decisions. For this reason, nobody was too fussy over what we were doing or where we were going if we stayed within earshot of Daddy's whistle. I remember the way he whistled through his fingers for us. The sound could pierce your eardrums. That was our call home, like calling a pair of old dogs that had gone astray.

But we were still kids, and kids do dumb shit sometimes, no matter how responsible they are. One day that lives in infamy, we needed more than a whistle. The one time we did something stupid, and they never let us live it down. Everywhere we went for at least a year, Daddy would get drunk and say, "Let me tell you what these young 'uns did." And Eric would get fighting mad because he knew what was coming. One dumb mistake overshadowed years of trying to do everything just right.

Flat playing ground is hard to come by in the mountains, but the trailer Eric grew up in had a piece of bottomland out back. It must have been used as farmland at some point, but we mostly used it as a playground for bikes and mischief. We spent hours out there, hours away from the close confines of a single-wide. The field provided us the space to talk and cuss without the listening ears of adults. In the corner closest to the trailer was a rusty, old, uncapped, metal pipe that made a guttural gurgling sound. I remember it being at least a couple of feet high. We spent hours throwing rocks, sticks, and whatever was lying around down that magnificent hole in the ground. When the wind kicked up, there would be a faint smell of gas emitting from the pipe, but at eleven, you don't think about what the smell means or what it can do.

When bike riding had lost its thrill and the blackness of that hole had perplexed us long enough, our investigation began. I started dropping things down it. We learned that it would make that splash at the bottom. I remember Eric saying, "We need to know exactly what's going on down there." And he went inside to get us a flashlight so we could investigate the situation further. He couldn't find a flashlight anywhere. But there was never a shortage of lighters, so he brought back a Zippo lighter. Square, smooth, silver, and shiny. It was perfect. We could strike it, and it would stay lit. It was the closest thing to a flashlight we could come up with. We lit it near the hole and bent over to look down inside.

All I remember is Eric striking the lighter, the flame appearing, and then that awful *boom*! A sound unlike any other I had ever heard. Immediately I smelled things burning, hair, fabric, and leaves. I looked over and saw Eric on fire. He dropped to the ground and began rolling around. I was so grateful for all the volunteer firefighter assemblies in school that taught us to stop, drop, and roll. A wave of panic and indescribable fear washed over me. I knew at that moment Eric was going to die. My face was hot, and I could tell something wasn't right with my eyes. I didn't realize then that the ends of my eyelashes were singed off, and I now had bangs that I didn't have before. Everybody came running. I don't remember if we hollered out or if they heard the boom. By the time they came, Eric had put himself out, and I had burned every inch of hair on my face and head. Finally, Daddy came running. The first thing he said was "Don't tell ye' mother!"

I had heard this before. He said that every time we got into something we shouldn't. He knew my mom would not approve of anything we did. But I wasn't sure how I was supposed to keep this particular incident a secret. I was positive my mom would notice the singed pieces of hair that framed my face. And she did, in fact, though I don't remember getting in trouble for it from her.

I think my dad was afraid of my mom in some ways—always afraid that she wouldn't let me see him if I ever got hurt. But I never got that impression. She never held visits over his head that I recall. Looking back, I see all the ways she protected me when it came to my dad. She would never tell me when he was coming to pick me up in case he didn't show. She always told me he loved me but that he was irresponsible. She helped me understand who he was and that his actions weren't a reflection on how he felt about me. She wrote off back child support, and I never heard her speak an ill word about him. There was plenty of material there she could have used. Instead, she cultivated and nurtured my relationship with him the best way she knew how. Even if that meant turning me loose again with no eyelashes or eyebrows.

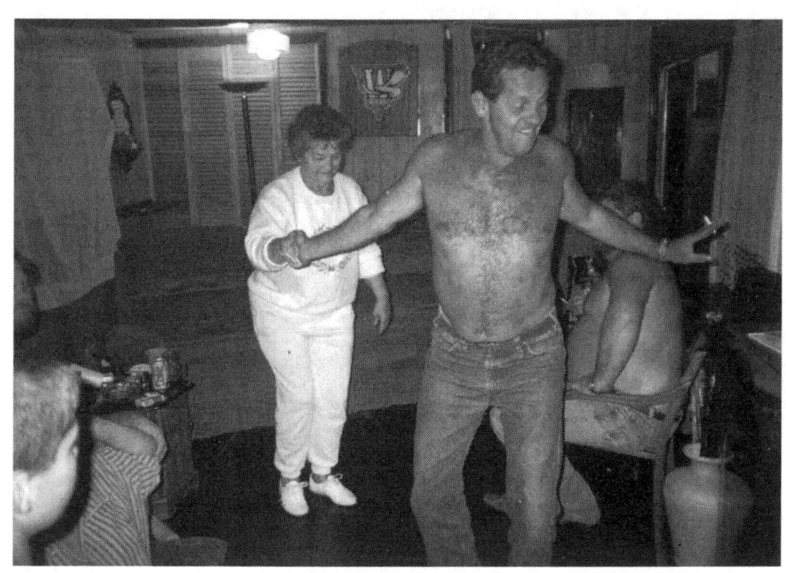

Dancing with Granny B

Water

1993

The majority of my childhood revolved around water. I mean a certain kind of water. A certain kind of freedom that felt like a vacation but wasn't a trip to the beach or the lake. Instead, it was the kind of place that was both tragic and beautiful. Follow a dirt road that had seen years of abuse toward places where salt-of-the-earth men who worked long hours for somebody else to get rich had long since gone. Some people call it mountaintop removal or surface mining. I've known them as strip jobs my whole life.

No matter what you call it, it is a disgrace. Moving and shifting, freezing and thawing, it took millions of years to create the ecological marvel that is central Appalachia and that humans managed to destroy in a hundred years' time. Gone are our mountaintops, which we will never see in their original form again. I've spent my fair share of time on strip jobs and can say that even with all the destruction, you can't deny the feeling of freedom and sense of wonder when you reach that flat expanse.

Hollers can feel suffocating, especially when you're a kid. On top of these mountains I could breathe, feel a breeze, look out over the beauty that is the Appalachian Mountains. The valleys looked different from up there. It made me proud of where I was from.

I don't know how my dad felt about it because he never said. I suspect he was up there to evade the law and any woman who frowned on his drinking all day. He'd take Eric and me up there to swim. Every strip mine around here is littered with ponds. Those ponds can be dark, soupy, or just the right shade of chocolate. At times I've seen them Bahamas blue to the bottom. Something should have told us it wasn't natural to swim in a pond you could see right to the bottom of on top of some mountain in eastern Kentucky, but we might not have listened. This was our retreat, even if these ponds were built to catch runoff or wash coal. In the mountains, we tend to make the best of every situation, and for us, this was like heaven, driving some dusty old road in the back of a pickup truck looking for this liquid oasis. I guess we never realized there was any other way.

Daddy would back his truck right up to the edge of the water, and we'd all get out. He'd crank up John Prine and throw his tailgate down. A cigarette hanging on his bottom lip like it was holding on for dear life. Digging around the cooler, the ice so cold it hurt my hands to reach inside. Budweiser can with water dripping off the edge. His legs would dangle, his shirtless back and chest already brown from years in the sun. He would laugh and throw his head back.

I know he had things that weighed on his mind. He had to. At the time, he seemed like he didn't have a care in the world. Eric and I would ease our way into the crystal-blue water. The bottom would be thick with clay and whatever else had settled out. I loved when we covered our faces with this gray conglomerate, like soldiers on a secret mission. Other times, we would see how far we could venture out before the water crept over our heads. We didn't go far before the bottom slopped to at least ten or twelve feet.

It was not an ideal swimming hole for a couple of kids. Eric still couldn't swim at eleven, so I never pushed the issue, but I longed to swim past the point of safety. Swim out to where I might never come back. At the same time, I wanted him to be safe. I knew he'd follow me. If growing up had been like swimming, where we knew right away when we were over our heads, maybe we wouldn't have gone so far.

Pond water was everywhere we went. Anytime I was near water, it seemed to quiet all the voices churning around. It gave me an inner peace. My favorite was probably the one that sat directly behind our uncle David's house at the head of Snow Lane in Caney. He lived on a piece of property that his family had mined, and what remained was a beautiful piece of flat land and a rock wall that rose fifty feet or better with a pond at the bottom. David's place was somewhere everyone was welcome. Doors open, Bob Seger blaring, a dark-green single-wide trailer, a POW flag whipping in the wind. Granny B would get up and dance with my daddy. He would twirl her around. They existed in their very own ballroom. We all existed in our own fantasy at Uncle David's.

The pond was there, and saw it all: every fish we caught, the poor water dogs we caged, and the nights we stayed awake when all the rest of the world was asleep. It was our go-to form of entertainment for years. It sucked in adults just the same as children. On summer days when the heat was unbearable, we would squeal with delight when David would jump in to cool off, even for a moment.

More often than they tried out our hobbies, though, we would participate in theirs. Like us sneaking beer out of the refrigerator in potato chip bags to run outside and drink. David built a floating platform that he named the pontoon—giant pieces of Styrofoam with a plywood deck nailed to the top. We could paddle it all around the pond for fishing and swimming. We never cared that it wasn't motorized.

Eric and I never could keep up with anything from one year to the next. My dad would buy us a new fishing pole and tackle box at the beginning of every summer. He'd spend all day floating around the pond at David's, teaching us how to fish and letting us try sips of beer. Eric wore a ball cap with a gold fishhook clipped on the bill, like you sometimes see at a gas station, right by the register. Both my dad and Uncle David filled in for Eric's dad, who never was around. I didn't mind sharing my dad. There were times when I thought Eric needed my dad more than I did. They were his heroes. Flawed as they were, worn out as that spot of land might have seemed, we found what we needed and never knew to want any different.

Eric and his dirt bike

Sunday

1993

The mining companies left miles of flattop mountains behind. Mountains that were once gently rolling peaks now looked like they had been sawed off, and the dirt and rock inside were exposed. It is almost impossible for vegetation to grow once you take the earth away. My family would spend all day on Sunday roaming through these hills from mountaintop to mountaintop, up and down through pond-sized mudholes, singing and riding.

I often wondered why Daddy would work six days a week in this desert landscape to spend his only day off roaming through reclaimed mine land. Eric and I usually rode in the back of Daddy's truck, but we loved it when he let us take turns driving. We'd sit up on the edge of the seat, our feet barely touching the pedals, and he'd teach us which path to take to keep from getting stuck. Lessons like these would be helpful later when he'd get too drunk to drive home, and we'd take the wheel. Eric and I never fought much. I always got him with "I'm the oldest" when it came to driving on the main road. I don't know which is worse to come across on a two-lane mountain road at night, a drunk or a twelve-year-old, but either one was likely. We loved that old Jeep pickup truck, faded black with orange and red stripes on the hood—big jacked-up tires for four-wheeling. Daddy loved nothing more than riding around in the hills, drinking Budweiser, with the music so loud you couldn't talk. Blasting the Rolling Stones, he sang with his whole body, moving like Mick Jagger. The door locks were black with a white stripe around the middle and a Playboy bunny in the center, slightly worn from pulling them up and down to lock and unlock the door, and he had replaced the rear bumper with a black metal pipe because something he hit tore the other one off.

All our trips started at Shot's Grocery, where he would get us a treat. Shot's was like all the other mom-and-pop stores that dotted the landscape. It was a simple block building with a couple of pumps outside. Shot and his wife lived in a house next door to the store. I would go for a Milky Way and a Mountain Dew in the little glass bottles. Eric would always pick Diet Pepsi and a Butterfinger.

"Why do you always get a Butterfinger? You end up having to pick that shit out of your teeth all day," I'd say.

With a grin, he'd say, "Nobody better lay a finger on my Butterfinger."

When I finished my pop, I would see if I could peel the Styrofoam label off in one piece and then stuff it down into the bottle.

The sign on the door said shoes and a shirt are required. This sign never applied to my daddy. If it was between May and August, he was not wearing a shirt, and nobody questioned that. After a fill-up and some ice for the cooler, he'd say, "You young'uns ready?" We knew this was our cue to sit down. I can still feel the wind on my face as we sat with our backs against the rear windshield, facing out and looking at the people who would pull up behind us. I always hated that my hair was so long that it stayed in my face and tangled in the wind. I was too young to put my hair in a ponytail on my own and too awkward to ask anybody to do it for me. A lifelong struggle to ask for help began here. Here during weekends with my dad. My mom took care of things like this without me having to ask. My dad didn't know. I never wanted to be too demanding or to inconvenience anyone. That left me with a rat's nest at the end of the day. As we wound our way around Pinetop's two-lane roads, the hills rose sharply up each side of the narrow valley. Daylight doesn't stick around long there. Sunlight finds its way in slowly.

A whole convoy of trucks would be behind us, including Eric's mom, Uncle David, and all of their friends. It was how everyone passed the time. And then there was the woman who trailed them all summer. She came bouncing down the road in a beat-up brown Chevette. We were in awe of anyone who goes four-wheeling in a Chevette, but a determined woman can conquer just about anything. Her pursuit was incessant, I'll give her that. When she caught up to us, she just left that old Chevette sitting in a mud hole and climbed right in our truck.

We seemed to spend all day on Sundays roaming around the hills. Now and then, when they'd find a good spot to stop, they'd let us out to run around while they got a beer and smoked. Then when the evening summer light began to fade on the mountain, we would make our way down, and I would have to return to another world. The world that was my life with my mom. That was different than the life Eric went home to, where they partied right on through the night. While I was home getting ready for school, he was still in it, even though it was Sunday.

Eric at David's pond

Summertime

1992

I never felt welcomed at my stepmom's house. I call it my stepmom's house because my dad seemed like only a guest there, making me feel like a guest there—an unwanted guest at that. She worked all the time, and I always thought she was annoyed I was there. That we were there. Anytime there was me, there was Eric. We were a package deal. So it was two kids to watch and feed. We tried to stay out of her way as much as possible by walking up and down the holler a lot. By messing around in the creek catching crawdads and setting minnow traps full of white bread. By doing whatever it was we did to keep from being inside.

"If we can catch enough, maybe Terry will take us up David's fishing."

I'd say, "Maybe," as I secured the rope to the bridge.

"Watch this," Eric would say, sticking his finger in the pincher of a crawdad and then slinging his finger around, trying to make it fly off. This made me uncomfortable. I would have never told him that. I never wanted to hurt any living things, and sometimes, as a kid, that makes you uncool.

Eric always had a four-wheeler or a dirt bike he was trying to get running. My mom never let me have anything like that. She thought they were dangerous, and my papaw thought they kicked up too much dust. So I reveled in the freedom I felt when we ripped up and down the old logging road behind my stepmom's house.

I never had a bedroom of my own when I was with my dad. He never really had a bedroom of his own either. He just had places where he stayed, which meant a lot of couch sleeping for me. My stepmom had two couches parallel to each other. They didn't match. They were the only things in the room besides a TV in an otherwise empty entertainment center. She wasn't big on interior design. She wasn't big on family. There were never any pictures on the wall or family photos sitting around. Just the necessities. She had Corn Pops, my dad's favorite cereal, that she kept on top of the refrigerator. And she made the best peanut butter fudge, which she poured onto an oval platter to let it cool. The smell of peanut butter and boiling sugar filled the kitchen. Hungry for a slice while it was still warm, I could taste it melting in my mouth, but I didn't dare ask. The comforting hum of the air conditioner that filled up the window, hanging over the edge outside, its constant cool breeze. I can muster fond memories of that time, but I always knew that the fudge and the cereal weren't there for me. Nothing in that house was there just for me.

My mom had a friend who worked at Kroger and boxed up everything she thought I'd enjoy and shipped them to me. Just for me. In a care package that summer, she sent me *Wayne's World*, a bottle of Sunflowers perfume, and a movie theater box of Junior Mints. Eric and I carried that VHS everywhere with us, watching *Wayne's World* until we could quote every line. My sun-kissed skin was hot from a day outside, cooled under a heavy homemade quilt, the only light in the room coming from the glow of the TV. At that moment, no matter what we had seen that day or how uncertain tomorrow might be, all was well on our piece of the Earth.

Before our innocence was lost. Before the drugs and alcohol. Before the pills. Those pills were God and Big Pharma's gift to all that ails the mountain man, which turns out was much more than his back. I want to write about the first time I did a pill. It was a turning point, one of those things you think you'll never forget. But I can't. I don't remember. I don't remember any of my first-time meetings with drugs except for OxyContin. I try to dig into early childhood, but I find myself writing about drugs, which would come to blur all those early memories.

It was my junior year of high school, and OxyContin was showing up everywhere—in the hallways at school, at parties on the weekend, and in medicine cabinets all over central Appalachia. I was with Eric the first time I did an OC. It was fall, and we were riding around in the hills when we came across a mutual friend. He was eager to share. OxyContin was unlike anything else. At that time, people were excited to introduce anyone they could find to this new drug. We sat in the cab of his truck and split a twenty-milligram pill between the three of us. I knew right then that's all I ever wanted. If I could feel that way for the rest of my life, everything would be okay. It would become a never-ending cycle, with specific memories sticking out more than others when I look back, but the first time was groundbreaking, life changing.

Why did I end up thinking about my first OxyContin when I was trying to remember being at my stepmom's house? Feeling in the way. Feeling too much. All roads led to one girl in one time dealing with emotions and feeling well beyond her capacity to grip.

Eric's bedroom

WBCR

1992

Eric and I bought microphones at Dollar General. We programmed them to play through the FM radio dial 88.9 from Eric's bedroom. We thought we were for real then. We could broadcast all our favorite classic rock songs, the latest weather, and sports, live from Branham's Creek. Life could not get any better than that.

We worked for hours coming up with the perfect playlist: Hendrix, Hank, and "Going Up the Country" by Canned Heat, which we were obsessed with. The entirety of sports news in Kentucky at the time was how Duke had just hit an unprecedented last-second shot to knock Pitino and his Wildcats out of a final-four spot. We were a state in mourning. This was the game that marked that team "The Unforgettables." We reported on the weather, which was basically the current condition outside Eric's bedroom window. It was cold that night, but the signs of spring were in the air. The days would get warmer, and it would cause me to get that itching feeling—that feeling you get when you've outgrown your winter skin and you're ready to break free. I feel it even now after a cold winter when I have to shake the frost. I know Eric felt it too. He didn't have to say so; I just knew. At eleven years old, we didn't have any inkling about what was happening in the world. Instead, we talked about who was dating whom or what we were looking forward to that summer, like any other preteens. Carr Creek Elementary was our life, so therefore, our news.

We had our studio set up on the bedroom floor, in front of Eric's stereo. Somehow, he had gotten his hands on one of those floor-model types with the big glass doors. He had traded something for it. Every time I went to his house, he'd have something new; he would have traded one thing for another. I always wondered how that came about. I never had anybody offering to trade me anything, but things were different at Eric's. I would have traded for one if the opportunity had presented itself. That thing stood three feet tall and had a radio, tape deck, and CD player, each with its own shelf, and space at the bottom for CDs. With that stereo, a chest, and bunk beds, there wasn't much room for anything else. So, there we'd sit, cross-legged on the floor on old, brown, worn-down carpet, with that big glass door open, radio notes in our laps. A real professional setup.

Between Eric's CD collection and whatever knowledge we thought we could bestow on the world, we did this in hopes that somebody driving down the road at that exact time would tune in to that exact channel and make us real-life radio personalities. The range for this magical device is long forgotten, but it was big enough to give us a slight chance to be heard.

The irony is that we were both painfully shy and avoided any situation where we had to be heard. Speak to either of us, and the heat rose from our necks into our faces. This kept me from speaking up; I sure didn't want any attention drawn to the fact that my face lit up like a Christmas tree whenever I had to speak. But it was different between us. We talked easily to each other, and that's all we ever needed. Most of the time, we didn't have to speak those needs at all. We had a connection. We were like a spirit that had been split in two. We both preferred being quiet and under the radar. That may be why this radio gig worked so well for us.

We never made the big time, but we entertained the crowd of grown-ups partying in the living room that night. The best part was running out to the car and listening to ourselves. There was something about capturing a moment like that—seeing or hearing how others see or hear you—that is compelling. Of course I didn't know I'd be sitting with these memories alone, all these years later. How I would love it if we could get our hands on those write-ups. Every day, I regret not taping those shows.

Saturday Nights and Sunday Mornings

1994

Waking up at Eric's house on Sunday morning, the sun would already be high in the air, the heat beginning to rise, light streaking through the windows and burning off the particles suspended in the air. All of Saturday night was beginning to fade, Bonnie Raitt playing loud and clean on the stereo, and my aunt Jenny would be cooking breakfast. Most of the time, she was making fried eggs. I preferred my eggs scrambled, but I never got the impression I had a choice. The doors were open, and the fresh air filtered in. She would be busy cleaning the house. Mixtures of stale smoke and Pine-Sol swirled through the air.

I would feel energized and safe. Everything seemed in its place. Standing in the doorway, the warm sunshine on my bare feet heating my entire body. Daddy would be in the driveway, tinkering with his truck, a black Jeep truck that was a legend among the cast of characters surrounding us. He was always tinkering with things; nothing seemed to suit his standards. There was always room for improvement. But, in the bright light of summer, everything seemed possible.

Just twelve hours earlier, the house was lit up, cars packed in the driveway, everybody from up and down the creek converging here at the trailer beside the road. As many people that packed in here on a Saturday night and as many chemicals as they ingested, nobody ever got mad, and nobody ever got sad. This was the happiest bunch of damn drunks I would ever see. It gave me a false sense of safety about house parties and a fantasy of what they would consist of. Most of the time, Eric and I would go to bed before things broke up.

We slept in Eric's room—black metal-tube bunk beds, a stereo, a chest of drawers, and sometimes a TV. There wasn't much room for anything else, but something about the smallness made it cozy and secure. We would lie there and listen to them talk and sing over top of the music. Vibrations from the dancing shook the whole house. The lights flickered when "Hearts for Sale" played. That song got ahold of my daddy, and he would spin the chandelier in the kitchen, causing it to short out. Eventually we slept, and in the morning, everybody would be gone.

As we got older, we were the ones up all night, vibrating the floor, singing over the music. It was our friends who crowded the driveway, who ganged up on Saturday night, still at my aunt Jenny's, still with my dad, still with the chemical companions. And it seems like we woke up one day, and everybody was gone. We had our last party, and we all went our separate ways. I don't remember telling anybody bye or how much they all meant to me. One day, it just stopped.

Five Miles

1994

Red, white, and gold cellophane-covered packages littered the floor, black garbage bags were bursting full. There were enough cigarette packs to make a person's chest hurt if they thought about it long enough. Eric and I sat cross-legged on the brown-carpeted floors of Uncle David's house for hours, cutting out the corners of each cigarette pack, careful to keep them intact, talking about what we might buy. Most everybody we knew smoked Marlboros for a good while, all to collect miles.

The Philip Morris company, makers of Marlboro, started that ingenious merchandise marketing program in the early 1990s. Each pack of cigarettes was valued at five miles. Those miles could be redeemed for a variety of outdoor-themed products. It was ironic. Our duty was to make sure every mile was counted. Our payment would be when we got to pick a garment from the catalog. The truth was, I never would have worn anything from that catalog out in public. It was 1994. I was in the eighth grade and at the height of embarrassment. Just existing was enough to make you stand out in middle school, and the last thing I wanted was to stand out. Those days, I was more into wearing Guess and Z Cavaricci. My friends would have given me pure hell over something like a Marlboro shirt. But Eric wore that shit proudly and often. Maybe it was easier for boys. Or maybe he had accepted that nobody would buy him name-brand jeans.

It's another thing I never mentioned to him. I wonder if we would have one day talked about it, if one day had come.

My life, unlike his, was compartmentalized. Being here at Uncle David's with my dad was only one storyline I was living out. During the week, I was home in Hale's Branch, going through the motions of a school week. I spent a lot of time at school because mom taught there—academic, speech, and basketball teams. There were nights when we would be the last ones at the school, locking the place behind us. When I was younger and Daddy couldn't keep me on the weekend, I stayed with a babysitter.

Babysitter feels like a generic term for a family that was much more than that. Imogene and Neil were a refuge for me. They were honest, consistent, and loving. Mom and Imogene were the same age. Imogene started keeping me when I was five months old and never stopped. She had just miscarried and was lost in the aftermath. My mom needed someone to keep me when she went back to work. Imogene and Neil became the model for a family I never had. In them, I saw what a loving, respectful marriage looked like. I saw what can happen when two people choose to live a life together, working toward the same goals. They took me on vacations, to dinner, and grocery shopping on weekends. They never searched for things outside themselves to make them happy. I spent a lot of time with Imogene and Neil, and I see now what that meant for me.

My puzzle had many pieces. Imogene and Neil were a puzzle piece. Life with Mom was a puzzle piece. Time with Dad was a puzzle piece. Eric's life seemed like a lot of the same. He didn't have respite. All his nights looked like Saturday. The same sort of piece that doesn't add up to a bigger picture.

Wild nights surrounded us our whole lives. The adults went on singing, drinking, and smoking, and we went on watching, learning, and listening. Eric and I talked about our future plans if we weren't scheming on how to sneak a beer. Eric's plans were always more of the immediate future, like finding a better guitar, a Fender he could trade his Sears guitar for. Or starting a band. I dreamed of going off to college somewhere away from eastern Kentucky. After watching *Rudy* one too many times, I desperately wanted to attend Notre Dame. Eric never talked about college or what he might do for a living.

We mostly talked about music and our passion for discovering new artists, and that's what drove us. That was the type of thing we lived for. I was heavy into the Grateful Dead and wore a lot of tie-dye. I would have loved nothing more than to go on the road with them, to become an official Deadhead selling grilled cheese sandwiches in the parking lot to earn enough cash to make it to the next show. Eric and I could talk the way you do when you're not self-conscious. The way you do when everything in the world is still new. The way you do when you're unfiltered and uninhibited by knowledge of the world. The way you do with someone who's family.

When we'd get those miles counted and tucked away safely in a Ziploc bag, we'd sit for hours making our final decision. All around us, miles burning lungs, miles going in the mouths that taught us how to talk. Miles and miles left to go, or so we thought.

BETTY
TRIPLETT'S BR.
FLOYD
KNOTT
80
MOUSIE
BALL FK
SOFTSHELL
JONES FK.
550
TOPMOST
GARNER
HOLLYBUSH
LEBURN
1697
KITE
NDMAN
PIPPA PASSES
160
REYNOLDS FK CH
SNOW LANE
IVIS BIBLE CH
MALLIE
BRANHAM'S CK
PUNCHEON
1393
SHOT'S GRO.
KNOTT
COLLINS BR
PINE TOP
ROPEWORKS
LETCHER
582
DEANE
15
REDFOX
COLSON
HALE'S BRANCH
ISOM
PERRY
LETCHER
7
15
WHITESBURG
BLACKEY

Aunt Jenny's Trailer

Peeling Apples

1994

I don't remember us ever asking what the appropriate age for Seagram and Sprite was, but I do recall that first sip, that first time I had a warm and fuzzy feeling. Alcohol brought a euphoria that washed over me. It felt like the edges had been softened. That sweet burning sensation as it hit my tongue, throat, and belly, burning all the way down.

The Seagram's bottle was clear glass, clear as the liquid inside—not like the brown bottles my dad usually drank. And the gin was clear like the Sprite, making it easy to conceal. The bottle had tiny knots all over it, making it hard to hold. It was Eric and me again on a summer Saturday night, left to entertain ourselves while the party rolled on. Eric stood lookout while I poured.

"Is that too much liquor? Reckon, what's the right pop-to-liquor ratio?"

"Hell, I don't know. Just hurry up before you get us caught."

"They don't care."

After a few sips, we felt the need to roam. I can't recall if we were drunk or just thought we should be. It was hard to tell at thirteen. It was always a fine line to experiment but not cross it and go too far, and we were beginning to get our feet wet.

Dovie lived across the road from the trailer Eric grew up in. I don't think we were kin, but she treated us like grandchildren. Dovie's house seemed like a mansion to me. With its paved driveway and carport, everything was so fancy and delicate on the inside. It was a single-story brick ranch with a barn out back. I never saw any animals there, but it sure made for an excellent place to hide and get into trouble. We'd sneak into the barn's loft and smoke hay.

Eric and his mom lived right off the road on Route 1393, past that curve that seemed to take everybody out. My aunt Jenny's trailer was brown and white with a front porch added on, covered on one end with a porch swing and a deck on the other. It had some age on it, but she worked hard to make it a home. The yard was small but always neat and well-maintained, with shrubs and flowers, which gave it color and a sense of pride. Everywhere we went, she looked for a start to dig up and take back to her yard. Elephant ears, ferns, rose bushes—whatever she could find. The occasional pot plant in a five-gallon bucket spray-painted green and hidden out back. One bedroom was on the right end, and one was on the left—a living room and kitchen in the center. Years later, I know that Dovie owned the trailer and the property. At the time, though, it was Aunt Jenny's. And as much time as I spent there, it felt a little bit like mine.

Dovie seemed old when we were kids, as far back as I can remember. Her hair was silver and long, way past her shoulders and closer to her waist. She always wore it up in a bun, tight and neatly stacked on top of her head. She'd have on that zip-up floral-patterned duster and white tennis shoes. I'd see her and her husband, Stanley, playing Rook at Granny B's in the wintertime.

I don't know why we thought going over there at two in the morning was a good idea, but that's what we did. Now it seems to me that the real question is why she was up that late. Her, in that metal folding chair, like the ones you see at a tent revival, pulled right up to the side of the road, peeling apples. She had a whole five-gallon bucket she had been working on most of the night.

The warm breeze of summer was blowing the smell of apples all around. As soon as we crossed the road, the smell of freshly peeled apples filled my nose. I had never before seen anybody peel an apple in one long piece, like a curlicue party decoration.

As far as I was concerned, she was the best apple peeler I had ever witnessed. We went right up, and she cut off a slice and handed it to us with her knife, then cut off a piece for herself and used her knife like a fork. I had never seen anything quite like it. Wallering that apple slice around in her mouth, she said, "Running around here after dark will make your pecker fall off."

Eric giggled nervously and said, "Ah, Dovie, you know that ain't true."

"Ask any man around here that thinks he can fool around after dark."

I shuffled around, eager to change the subject. "What are you doing with all these apples?"

"Young'uns, I'm fixing to make a mess of pies."

I was not eating any pie she made because of the one time she fed Eric hog brains and told him it was scrambled eggs. Old folks were always trying to get us to believe something crazy.

She never let on if she knew we were drinking. She didn't have to peel apples in the middle of the night, but she was nosy. Maybe she only did this so she could make sure she knew everything happening across the road at Eric's house. She'd come bright and early the next morning, being as loud as she could, knowing the whole bunch was hungover. She'd bust through the door, never offering to knock, and say, "Get up, y'all. It's time for church." Then she'd laugh, knowing good and well none of that crowd had seen the inside of a church since their mommies made them. But she never lectured them or asked why they insisted on spending all this time drinking and partying. That's just who they were; everybody knew it and let them be.

That was the first night we had Seagram's and Sprite, but it wouldn't be the last. Maybe because of that first time and maybe because of the strangeness of seeing Dovie peeling apples in the middle of the night, we always remembered it. Later, it was some sort of shorthand for us. Eric would look at me and say, "Peeling apples," and we would both lose it. Remembering those early days where we still felt safe and looked after, odd as it was.

ADDICTION
1997–2004

Mandi washing the Jetta

Freedom

1997

My first car was a bright-red, four-door 1991 Volkswagen Jetta with a crank-back sunroof. Some may be too young to remember a crank-back sunroof. A handle was attached to the headliner that you had to roll back, similar to manual windows. Most of my friends had cars with automatic windows, but, to me, this was just one of the many Jetta quirks. I washed it so often that my papaw told me I would wash the paint right off. It was clean, but it wasn't the most reliable. Sometimes it would get me out and then not start back up at the most inopportune time, like when I drove over to Balls Fork to buy pot. This car had some sixth sense that I was somewhere I shouldn't be. Nonetheless, it was my ticket to freedom, and boy, did I wear it out.

This wasn't the car I learned to drive in. Most of my driving expertise came from excursions in my mom's 1990 Chrysler minivan to and from Squire Watts grocery at the mouth of my holler. I'd wait around, hoping she'd send me down to the store for cigarettes or pop. Early on, I felt the freedom a car could bring. I was never afraid. I've always been confident behind the wheel. She acquired the van after totaling our other car driving home drunk from the bar. She needed a car she could buy outright to keep the price of insurance down after the accident. An interior design store in Hazard was selling their delivery van, so my mom got it cheap. It was a cream-colored, wood-paneled van with "Paper Patch Interiors" painted on the side in faded pastel lettering. Peak embarrassment for my seventh-grade self.

There was no money for a new paint job, and I knew we were lucky to have a car to drive. She covered the back window in a "No Fear" sticker, a T-shirt brand popular in the early nineties, which complemented Marilyn Manson's face and Grateful Dead bears on either side. I'd been driving for what seemed like years by the time I got my license.

Whenever I had extra money, I would make the trip to Vicco. Vicco's name comes from the Virginia Iron Coal and Coke Company, and it's one of the dozens of coal mining towns that seemingly arise out of nowhere, dotted along the landscape of eastern Kentucky. My destination was Ritchie's used car lot, where Eric bought a white Camaro sometime later. Ritchie's also happened to be our local head shop, and I was always in the market for a new Grateful Dead sticker.

There was a small, white double-wide trailer converted into an office with ten or twelve cars on the lot. Some dude sat behind a metal desk, leaning back in a broke-down office chair. Racks of band shirts, keychains, and air fresheners filled the unused floor space. It was nontraditional in its arrangement: you could buy a car and a pipe all at the same counter. Eventually, I bought a sticker of every variety and covered every inch of rear window space on the Jetta with them. I wanted my car to look like the people who followed the Dead around the country. I'd never seen them live. I didn't live close enough to a major city. By the time I could drive, Jerry Garcia was dead.

Newly mobile, Eric and I were always looking for somewhere secluded to burn a joint. We drank a little on the weekends and smoked some after school, but it felt recreational and fun, not like we had to have it. One of our favorite spots was the graveyard behind Reynolds Fork Church. Because of the terrain in eastern Kentucky, most graveyards sit straight up and down on a hillside, and this one was perched on top of a mountain. It is nothing short of a miracle how funeral directors and trailer salesmen work their magic around here.

I'll never forget Eric showing me this place. We backed the Jetta in so we could see what was coming up the hill, and cranked up the sunroof and the radio. In 1991, this car came with a cassette deck, but I had a CD player installed to accommodate technological advancements. I carried my CDs in a black leather binder. They were arranged in alphabetical order by band, with the liner notes. While Eric worked on lighting a prerolled joint, I got the binder and flipped straight to the *Ps*, scanning for the bright prism colors of Pink Floyd's *Dark Side of the Moon*.

At sixteen, we didn't have the extra cash for a whole bag of pot, so we'd linger around outside the local pool hall until someone asked us if we wanted to buy a joint. The guys who played pool every day at the Pinetop Pool Hall were older than us. Eric had played pool and smoked pot here before when he spent the night with Justin, who lived across the road. Even though I was older, I was still cutting my teeth on this world. This was more Eric's world than mine.

We were so awkward, we couldn't even buy our own drugs. When you know your face will give you away, it makes it hard to initiate conversation. I preferred observation in these moments. I preferred observation in most moments. But these guys knew we weren't here to shoot pool. We didn't even get out of the car. Eric would roll down the window and motion for Clem to come over. Clem spent all his time at the pool hall, perfecting his combination shot, which he later used on some unsuspecting opponent. It is still unbelievable how he made all his money traveling from town to town, hustling people.

Clem leaned into the car, singing random lyrics by Cypress Hill or Insane Clown Posse. Then he said, "I just got back from Lexington. I took first at Shooters and brought home five hundred dollars."

"No shit!"

Pulling his hair back into a ponytail, he said, "That bunch down there only thinks they can play."

The whole time I'm thinking, "Can we get on with this?"

"Are y'all looking for something?"

Eric would mumble, "Yeah, man, you got a joint?"

Clem would whip a baggie out of his leather coat, flipping it so it unrolled and reveal a sack full of prerolled joints.

"I'm your ice cream man. Take your pick," he would say. Every damn time.

As we took turns inhaling and exhaling, passing it back and forth, the car filling with skunky smoke, I could feel the tension behind my eyes release. For a moment, I wouldn't have to worry about what would happen if my mom caught me. Or my grades at school or the fact that nobody ever asked me out when everybody else had someone to go out with on Saturday night. I was there in my car, without all the pressure. My senses became more attuned to the world around me. I could tell that my spirit and Eric's were more at ease. I practiced the art of exhaling out of my mouth while simultaneously inhaling through my nose. My dad liked to do this trick when we were kids to make us laugh. Smoke poured out of my body like a waterfall. Eric didn't even give this a second look. This was a party trick he'd seen every time I had a buzz for the last two years.

Every time we got stoned, we'd start coming up with big plans for the weekend. Passing me the joint held tightly between his thumb and first finger, the plans would roll into action. "If we can bum enough money at school this week, Mom can get us a keg. We can take it up Ropeworks."

I inhale deeply and answer with a chest full of smoke, "We could party at the switchback."

Eric would flip through the liner notes and come up with some pearl of wisdom: "You ever notice how you have to listen to this album from start to finish? How one song carries over to the next one?"

I sing the lyrics of Pink Floyd's "Breathe."

We stepped out of the car to get a closer look at the tombstones. He pointed out the fact that our grandpa is buried here. Our grandpa died in a car accident at thirty, long before either of us was even a thought. We had heard so many stories through the years, almost like he held some legendary status, but no one ever told us who he was. No one told us what music he listened to or what his favorite meal was. No one ever told us what kind of father he was. We only had a small stack of photos from his time in the navy and a few with his kids. It was all stories. Like how he died five miles down the road from where we were standing in that steep curve just below Ivis Bible Church. Like how he was drinking and maybe racing, and someone said it was raining. No one ever sat us down and told us anything. It all felt like hearsay, even if it was our family history. I never knew, until that day getting high at the cemetery, where he was buried. In the Fugate plot. When my dad and aunt Jenny would catch us drinking or smoking, they would say, "Well, they're Fugates." It was a legacy we thought we had to carry on.

If I ever came up here as a kid, I can't remember. It was peaceful there, overlooking the valley and homes below, tall trees towering over, and barely any room for the sun to peek through. There was a carpet of moss growing over most of the ground. An old rough lumber shelter built up on one side hung over the hill. I can picture a time when it was filled with families mourning the loss of their loved ones. Preachers and funeral home directors gathered around, heads down, the drone of hymns echoing through the valley. The boards are gray and weathered, and it looks like it couldn't bear the weight of another soul setting foot on it, or the whole thing would tumble like a house of cards. The weight of all that sorrow was dragging it down. Grandparents, great-grandparents, and uncles—all right here. And there we were, carrying on as the next generation of Fugates, the best we knew how.

The Whore from Hardburly

1998

When I hear "Papa Was a Rolling Stone," I am reminded of my dad. He went through phases with women and never committed to lasting relationships. He just kept women around out of necessity. It was hard to tell where he stood with women. Like Donna, who he was with for years after my mom. Sometimes he lived with her, and sometimes he lived where he could. It seems like he craved the presence of others but spent most of his life alone.

Eric probably knew better than I did about the flings he kept to himself on nights I wasn't around, but there was one that slithered through the cracks. After all these years, etched like a bad Polaroid in the gray matter of my mind. During this time, my daddy was living in motels or in his truck. Nothing says domestic bliss like two polyester-covered queen beds with a table and a straight-back chair. It was the mid-nineties, when opiates were beginning to make their way into the hollers of our small town. I can't be sure that's why Daddy was choosing to shack up with some woman in a seedy motel, but I can say that in all his years of drinking, he had never ended up here.

She had a tattoo that started above her knee and slipped up her thigh. It was the outline of a dragon, with no color, just black ink winding around. I never saw her in much more than cut-off Levi's shorts and a tank top, that dragon always peeking out from beneath. She was one of those people who still looked dirty even after she took a shower. There was something about her that water couldn't wash away. Scars that would stay with her forever. Pale and thin, with piercing blue eyes that made her look like she was staring right through you. That was probably from OxyContin.

I couldn't understand Daddy's desire. It overwhelmed him to the point of risking his relationships with all his family and friends to spend time with a woman who didn't seem that impressive. Seventeen at the time, I didn't try to understand. It was hard not knowing where he was—not knowing if he was safe—not knowing where to call if I wanted to talk to him. And he assumed my mom was taking care of things with me. It didn't seem like he cared or wondered if I was alright. He had never been around for any of my basketball games, speech tournaments, academic meets, or awards nights. He said he'd be there, but he never came. I used to watch for him out of the corner of my eye as I played, but I gave that up a long time ago. He just wasn't dependable. And I knew that.

The night Granny B died, my cousin Amber had to track him down in one of these motels to break the news. Granny B was not a fan of Lois, so he hadn't spent much time with her in the weeks leading up to her death. Granny B was the glue that kept us all together. After her death, things changed. Holidays and weekends changed. We struggled to get together as a family, and something felt incomplete when we did. The sense of security was gone. I felt it most for Eric. Our grandma was his protector.

After her funeral, we took Daddy's truck and a six-pack up a gas well road behind her house. Eric didn't say much, but I knew he was worried. She was the one who made sure he had what he needed. Her death was a turning point for both of us. My parents were wrapped up in their own lives. And now Eric had no one to keep him on the right path. I don't think he ever processed that grief. At that point, it felt like we were both left to fend for ourselves. No one was watching. Eric and my aunt

Jenny moved into Granny's house after she died. It became the place where we all partied. No more bologna sandwiches and candy bars. It was a high school *Animal House* every weekend. It was weird getting high and passing out around all the things that provided comfort when we were kids. We smoked pot in the kitchen and snorted coke in the bathroom next to her bottle of Red Door perfume and flower shower curtain. We didn't have Christmas or Easter there anymore.

After Granny B's death, Daddy didn't talk much about his lady friend. I guess he got tired of her, and that's when he moved back in with his third wife. And that was that, like nothing had ever happened. He went back to her house, but things felt different. This woman became a part of his past, but I could see her impact. Oxys were still new, and I hadn't been around them much. I knew exactly what it looked like when Daddy was drunk, but not what it looked like when he was on pills.

There wasn't much my daddy did that didn't have something in it for him. And that's what I think about that whole situation with her. Since the opioid surge, I see women like her all the time. I feel bad for her. She probably needed him just as much as he needed her. I can't blame her. After my own struggles with substance use and dysfunctional relationships, I have a better understanding. People do what they must do to survive.

Coal Camp Cocaine

1998

When Bert put the gun on the seat as he opened the door to get out, I knew this was a different situation. I cut my wide eyes over to Eric as he said, "Use this only if you have to. I'll be right back." At this point, I thought we might be in over our heads, but I didn't say it. We were young and needed dope. We had already traded anything we had from our bedrooms that was worth selling for drugs. The only thing I had left to offer was a reliable, legal means of transportation. That came in handy for transporting a drug dealer on a run.

We had been buying drugs from this guy for a couple of years now. His whole family made a living selling dope. We were dealing with the second generation in the business. They all lived together in a group of trailers beside the road in the holler close to where we grew up. A group of brothers making their living by providing to the community. It was genius in a way. They each sold a different drug to keep from falling out with one another. Going to school with their kids, I don't remember them ever saying a word about what their parents did for a living. Somehow, in this situation, our family name gave us clout. To some people, that might have meant they wouldn't sell us drugs. For these guys, it meant we could be trusted. And we knew enough about their family and their crazy shit—burning cars, shooting down powerlines, and shooting each other—that we should have feared them. What we feared was being seen there, because people only went there for one reason. But we cared about dope more than our reputations, so here we were.

When we bought dope there, we'd pull over at a wide spot in the road, across from the compound. This was the designated waiting spot. I would nervously wait in the car while Eric walked across the road to get dope. He was always the buyer. I always stayed in the car. We did this at least twice a week, and every time, I worried.

I imagined a swarm of DEA agents swooping in from all sides, blocking the road, guns drawn, knocking down doors, and yanking me out of the car for questioning. Would they notice we were kids? Barely old enough to drive. Would they care? Other times, I imagined a fate worse than the DEA—my mother. If she had rolled up on this scene, I would have preferred dealing with law enforcement.

I could tell if Eric scored by the way he walked back to the car. Not walking but not running either. A pace somewhere in between. A "let's get the hell out of here" gait. His Jenco jeans wide and sweeping back and forth, his favorite T-shirt—the one he got from the Family Values Tour up around Louisville. That was one of the few times he got out of here—a weekend in the city that he always talked about. As he got closer to the car, I could see we were out of luck.

"They're out," Eric said, "but if we take Bert to Wheelwright, he said he'll give us some." I knew the risk that was involved and what it would mean if we were seen with anyone from this family, whether we had dope in the car or not. What they did was no secret. It was all they did, so riding somewhere with them meant immediate guilt by association. But I also knew we needed cocaine. They didn't have any, but we could make it possible. That's when we headed out—three in the front seat of my S-10 pickup. Eric sat in the middle, which I was grateful for. It wasn't that I was afraid of Bert, but there is an intimacy that comes with sitting three deep in a pickup—a level I didn't want to experience. It took us about thirty minutes to get to Wheelwright from Knott County. Lynyrd Skynyrd's "Second

Helping" is thirty-seven minutes long. We rode across those mountains and winding back roads with the windows down.

For me, the waiting was a part of the high. We had a clear view of the house, which sat up on a hill in a row of houses that all looked the same. As I sat there staring at that row of dirty white clapboard houses, two rooms downstairs and two rooms upstairs, I thought about Wheelwright. It was an old coal town, and these were coal camp houses—likely built in the twenties for miners who worked close. In those days, miners were provided housing and paid in a currency known as scrip. The scrip could only be used in the company store or for services provided on company property. This went on for many years, essentially making the miners indentured servants. Their labor was exchanged for goods and shelter. In the long run, this would only benefit the company. The miners had no means of saving or working toward ownership. They often worked long, hard hours in unsafe and unregulated conditions. As a result, many men and children working in those mines had a fatalistic attitude toward their health. Death emanates every time they enter those mines. So, time spent away from the mine was lived to the fullest. Sitting there, waiting to score cocaine, I remembered reading that today's fatalistic habits of people from the mountains most likely started during this time—the first of many extraction industries that preyed on the people of central Appalachia. Disposable people fueled the industrial revolution, making everyone involved rich in many ways—everyone but themselves, their children, and the generations to come who would pay the price of mineral wealth.

As familiar as the terrain looked, I was still out of my comfort zone.

I knew about buying fifty bags or the occasional gram if we had the money, but I didn't understand why we needed a gun or how much dope we were talking about. We waited for what seemed like forever before Bert came back and threw a softball-sized bag on the dashboard, and off we went. No one mentioned an elaborate method to conceal this felony-sized sack we were now transporting. Bert didn't seem to mind. This was his every day. I wouldn't even be able to tell this to anyone when I showed up for AP biology on Monday morning and everyone talked about their weekends. I knew enough to know that. They'd all be talking about how they missed curfew because they'd stayed out too late splitting a six-pack of Zima in a parked car with some guy. I envied their ability to be content with that.

So, this is where our drugs came from. I could tell Bert had made this trip before. He would take this bag of coke home, cut it with some innocuous substance, and at least double his money. And we trusted him, week in and week out, putting up our noses whatever he cooked up at home, like a kid with a chemistry set.

But that night, we were snorting as pure a cocaine as comes out of Wheelwright. We were equipped with more than we could ever afford. We got high. Real high. Rubbing it on our gums. Big fat white lines. Licking residue off a CD case. Some Tony Montana *Scarface*–type shit. Eric told me he could always tell when I snorted cocaine because my right eye would droop. It was my tell. And people could read me if they knew, like poker players around a card table.

After we dropped Bert off, I remember heading straight to Ropeworks. We always went to Ropeworks to do our dope. It was safe and secluded. We could have gone back to my aunt Jenny's, which was probably the safest bet, but I knew Eric didn't want to be around his mom. It wasn't a thing for me to get high around her; I never thought twice about it. But she wasn't my mom. I remember all the times we sat in the car up there, listening to music and talking to keep from going home. Times that weren't parties, when it was just us. We should have been out doing everyday teenage things. Dates, ball games, or sleepovers. I hate it for us now. At that moment, though, on that mountain listening to Black Sabbath while we snorted line after line, drinking beer and doing Xanax to start working on coming down before the comedown started, I was content and didn't want those other things. Here, I didn't feel like an outsider. I didn't feel the pressures of relationships.

This was it. This was our routine. I don't think we thought about it being a problem. Nobody ever used the word *addiction.* Cocaine was a regular occurrence for us most weekends. I don't know about Eric, but I could never sleep on nights like those. My mind would race, and so would my heart—alive with thoughts and ideas.

I never told anybody about my first cocaine nosebleed. The tickle of liquid running down my face annoyed me enough to get me out of bed. I thought my nose was running from whatever they had used to cut the coke with, so one good nose blow should take care of it. The house was dark and quiet. Everyone else was able to fall asleep and shut off their minds. It wasn't uncommon for me to be the last one out and the first one up.

We were at Eric's house, where we all gathered to party or pass out. I went to the bathroom and realized blood dripped from my nose and down my face. A part of me was scared. This wasn't typical. But a part of me relished the idea. It was that part of my brain that was triggered during use. It was the part that thought this was cool, and if people could have this experience, they would understand. They wouldn't think it was concerning. I felt like a rock star, not like some kid looking for a way to numb her face and pain. This was my prom. My star performance. My first date. Cocaine was a drug I felt like I could do and then sleep off and go about my business.

But when opioids became our drug of choice, it seemed like that option was taken away. When we didn't have pills, we were physically sick. We needed the drug to maintain some normalcy. At that point, I could see the shift in the desperation that became a part of our routine. It didn't feel carefree anymore. We didn't take the time to wander around Ropeworks. I don't think we even enjoyed each other's company as much. It was all about avoiding being sick. We wouldn't even bother trying to find a safe place to get high. As soon as we scored, Eric would start busting up the pills. Opiates had left us shells of who we once were. We just existed together.

Ropeworks Senior Skip Day

Ropeworks

1999

Senior Skip Day felt like a rite of passage, except I skipped every year, regardless of my grade. Some parties are worth the risk. When 1999 rolled around, it was my opportunity to cut legally. Well, as a senior, it was at least acceptable to cut. The whole class had decided to have a bonfire and a few beverages at our favorite getaway, Ropeworks Branch. It had been my road to freedom to drink beer and smoke weed. It is even where I contemplated ending it all when things got to be too much, when the dark place got too dark and there was no sign of light. It may have seemed like any old holler road to most, but for me, it was an everyday escape from the uncertainty of adolescence. Following each curve where the road goes from asphalt to gravel, past all the houses to the very end, where the road ascends high on the mountain. The mountains seemed peaceful and safe; you couldn't see all the damage drugs were doing. You couldn't see the families struggling to survive. A whole population was hanging on to their history and love for the land. It seemed only fitting to bring everybody here for one last hoorah during our senior year of high school.

We started early that morning, prepping for what was sure to be the greatest night of our lives, and a part of me still craves that anticipation of something about to happen. When you planned a party, you just never knew what would go down, who was coming, who would hook up with who, who would pass out first—and, of course, there would be drugs. What kind of drug would we get into that night? But back then, things were different. I was different—carefree and uninhibited. Eric and I brought along two thirty packs of Busch Light, not because it was our favorite but because it was just the cheapest possible way to have sixty beers that didn't taste like complete shit.

The ride there was electric. It was May, so it was starting to get warm but was chilly enough at night for a fire. Deftones blaring, windows down, and that disconnected feel of a morning joint just calming enough that I didn't bust out of my skin with excitement. During that drive, it was as though my car knew the way. I began to zone out and contemplate my next move, how I would go on to college in Pikeville and start my life away from here. Graduation felt like the end of an era. Everyone was so full of dreams and aspirations. The reality was that most of us would be back home within a year. Some would never summon the courage to test the waters of leaving home at all, never venturing outside the safe embrace of the mountains.

From a two-lane asphalt road, I turned right to a one-lane asphalt road, then right again onto Ropeworks Branch. At the mouth of the holler, there was a small single-wide trailer where a woman cut hair. This turnoff was the scene of one of my many crimes, which, unbeknownst to me, was being closely monitored by my homeroom teacher. While he was getting a haircut, I stole the street sign right off its pole in broad daylight. It was green and shiny in all its glory, with the words *Ropeworks Branch* in white. It would be perfect for my collection. In my defense, I felt like I needed this souvenir to truly capture my love of this place. He reminded me on Monday in homeroom that stealing county property was, in fact, illegal, and I might want to rethink taking things of that nature in the future. "Lord," I thought, "don't let the county come to my house." My room was filled with stop signs, street signs, and road cones, each a small token to remember the night before. I would go to jail if they ever decided to visit me.

As we drove up the holler, everybody out in the yard and on the front porch waved. Everybody around here waved—didn't matter if you knew the person or not. It was a modest row of houses. Some people I knew, some I didn't. Then, right before the road began to go up the mountain, there was an old, abandoned white clapboard house, overgrown with kudzu vine and weeds so high there was no distinguishable yard. For no particular reason, the sight of this place sent shivers down my spine. Maybe it was the pot that made me feel this way. Maybe it was the kudzu and how it engulfed the house and its memories—knowing that someone had been there but not knowing their reason for leaving. So I always sped up there and avoided looking in that general direction. We didn't go to the top that night. We stopped at the switchback.

At the top, you could see for miles. Row after row of mountaintops that looked like knees scraped, leaving scars on the skin. We decided on the first switchback, just before the road meanders sharply up the mountain and just far enough out of sight. Out of sight of the people on their porches, although I doubt we were very discreet. Eric and I were the first ones on the scene. The first thing we did was build a ring of rocks and collect firewood. That ring of rocks kept us from burning the whole holler down that night. We carried rocks, one by one, from all over, but I mainly remember it being from the foot of the high wall, left after they finished strip mining. We selected them carefully by shape and size and made that giant ring. We always said, "No respectable party can exist without the perfect ring of rocks." As we carried rock after rock, I wanted to tell him that our lives would never be the same. I was leaving, and he was staying, and for the first time in our lives, we wouldn't be in the same town. I wasn't sure how things would change from here.

But I didn't.

I didn't say anything I was feeling at the time. And I still don't on most days, but I'm trying to take a chance, even though the vulnerability makes me feel like I could blow at any minute.

I still firmly believe in a ring of rocks and a good fire.

One by one, everybody filed in. Cars roared down the road, kicking up dust, and soon, we had a lineup of cars and trucks.

Juniors, seniors, and graduates, it didn't matter. We were there with one common goal: to make the most of what was left of our time together. Even then, I sensed we were in a shift. Never again would this group of people sit around drinking, smoking, laughing, and singing. Soon we would all move in a different direction. As I looked around at this hopeful crew, some of whom I had known since preschool, I didn't think I truly understood how special moments like these would become. We were on common ground as we sat on tailgates, legs dangling, sipping, smoking, and peering into the fire. We were all one. Sixty beers later, as evening turned to night and night turned to morning, the ashes began to smolder, I got in the car, cracked the windows, and leaned the seat back. Tonight, I'd sleep right there.

BETTY
TRIPLETT'S BR.
FLOY
KNOTT
80
MOUSIE
BALL FK
SOFTSHELL
JONES FK.
550
TOPMOST
GARNER
HOLLYBUSH
LEBURN
1697
KITE
NDMAN
PIPPA PASSES
WHE
160
REYNOLDS FK CH
SNOW LANE
IVIS BIBLE CH
MALLIE
BRANHAM'S CK
PUNCHEON
1393
SHOT'S GRO.
KNOTT
COLLINS BR
PINE TOP
ROPEWORKS
LETCHER
582
DEANE
15
REDFOX
COLSON
HALE'S BRANCH
ISOM
PERRY
LETCHER
7
15
WHITESBURG
BLACKEY

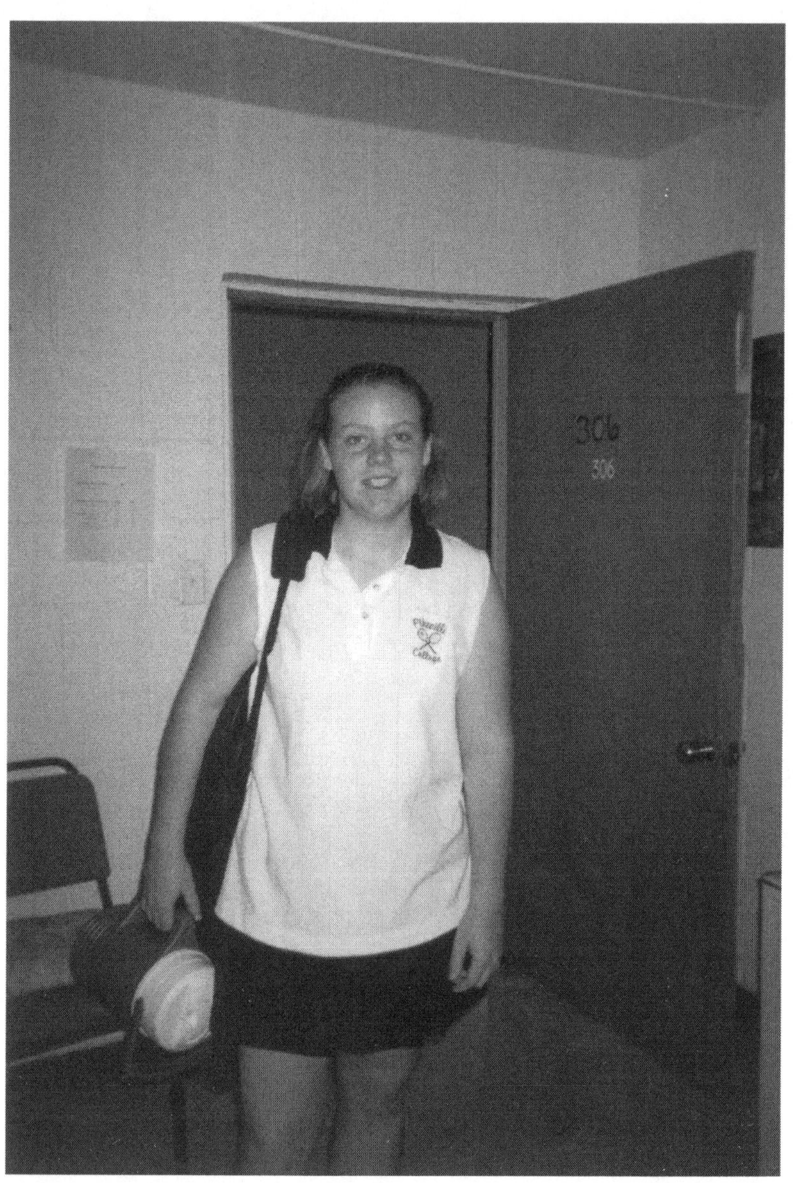

Mandi at Pikeville College

Pikeville College

1999

When I went away to Pikeville College, I was fifty-five miles from Red Fox, Kentucky. It might as well have been an eternity away. I was there on a tennis scholarship. Mom would call and say, "Mandi, they have classes there. It's not a country club." I thoroughly enjoyed myself, partying at the tennis house and smoking pot out of my dorm room window. I had always enjoyed a level of freedom that most kids our age didn't have. I had never been confined, never had a curfew or school-night restrictions. Everybody here was going crazy living out on their own for the first time. Here, my mom wouldn't be waiting up to check my eyes and smell my breath. The campus felt like it was vibrating, all those twentysomethings just looking for an outlet.

My dorm was set up like a suite with a living area, four bedrooms, and a bath. The walls were concrete block and painted institutional beige. The floor was a cold, hard tile. The bathroom looked like what I had always imagined a jailhouse bathroom might look like—two shower stalls with a curtain. A couple of toilets, surrounded by metal walls, looked like the school toilets I had avoided using my entire life. Sinks with mirrors made of reflective plastic. I guess we couldn't be trusted with real glass. This building hadn't had a facelift in a while, and it showed. Horribly modest at this juncture, I dreaded sharing a bathroom with eight other people. My roommates were from all over Kentucky, Virginia, and Ohio. I clicked right away with a couple of girls from Virginia.

Ashley and April were best friends already and lived just over the state line. This was my first experience making friends with people I hadn't known my whole life. I never had to make friends growing up in a small town—people know you because they've always known you. Now I didn't know who to be. I didn't know what would make others like me. Nobody knew my parents or even cared, for that matter. Being deep in the drug scene, it was clear that this was my focus early on. The thought that I might be screwing up some great opportunities never crossed my mind.

We all traveled back and forth a lot going home. It wasn't homesickness drawing us back; we needed the connections. April was the youngest of three; her dad was raising her. Her mom died of cancer when she was younger. Her scars were visible to me. Her whole family had scars that were visible to me. She partied like she was running from something. Her entire family partied like they were running from something. You could tell there was a hole they were all trying to fill. Ashley was the oldest of two, her parents were still happily married, and it seemed her home life was about as happy as anybody's I had known. Their hometown looked a lot like Hindman. I always felt welcomed there.

Like Hindman, Buchanan County was one of the areas of central Appalachia targeted by the Sackler family of Purdue Pharma. Their aggressive marketing campaign focused on areas with high-volume prescribers to boost the OxyContin market. All the while, they were pushing a false narrative to steer patients away from safer alternatives. Consequently, our communities were flooded with a highly potent, highly addictive narcotic. One that Purdue-trained sales reps were touting as having a less than 1 percent addiction rate. And so, we traveled the one-lane central road running through southwest Virginia like a vein running through the ever-present mountains, hollers like branches extending out where homes were tucked away, unphased by the outside world.

April had a black Mazda RX-7 with a stick shift. The way she drove that car was something like a dance, always too fast, with the music too loud. We would wind around curves, and she would shift and accelerate just as "Whiskey in a Jar" was hitting its stride. I felt like we were part of some greater consciousness that no one else could ever understand. We were looking for April's sister; she was our connection to OxyContin. Her sister was two years older than us and much further along the road of addiction. She was living in an apartment complex in their hometown. When we found her, there was hardly any furniture, just a couch, a TV, and a coffee table. The rooms were thick with smoke, but everything was spotless. She was living with a roommate, and when they came to the door, it looked like they had been working out, both in shorts and bras. It was close to Halloween, but you could tell they still had their air conditioning on. Something was burning these two up.

On the way there, April told us that her sister and her roommate never paid for drugs or for their apartment. Apparently, a close friend was a trust fund baby, and he kept them up in return for sexual favors. This apartment had more pills than I had ever seen in one location—Ziploc bags full. They had a bag for each, separated by milligram, in yellow, pink, and green. They had moved past crushing up OCs and snorting them. They were shooting them, and they invited me to.

I was eighteen, and it was my first semester of college. I was the senior class vice president of my high school. I graduated with a GPA higher than 4.0. I was a tennis standout. I was not supposed to be someone who struggled with substance use. But I had walked the line between two lives for a while now. Something about the alternative lifestyle was much more appealing to me than being a student-athlete. Kurt Cobain and Chris Cornell did drugs. They shot heroin. It was the nineties; heroin chic was everywhere you looked. I longed to be a waif Calvin Klein model.

So, I did it. I shot dope in an unfurnished apartment with my roommate's sister, whom I had just met.

I picked a needle out of a blue Walmart shopping bag. It was full of needles, still in the packages. This gave me a sense of security. It seemed like they were being safe. April's sister led me upstairs to the bathroom and told me to sit on the toilet. She assured me that everyone was nervous the first time and that she would shoot me up. This was also fairly common for first-timers.

The bathroom was plain and small. Everything was off-white. A sheen of sweat beads glimmered on her forehead as she bent down close to me. She was high. Her pupils were small, and she seemed to look right through me. Laying the pill on the bathroom sink, she covered it with a dollar bill and crushed it with a pop lid. The pill crunching on the counter sounded like tires on gravel, and I could smell the lemon Lysol they used to clean the bathroom.

Everything was about to change.

She placed the powder on the bottom of a pop can and started to heat it from underneath. It bubbled and mixed with the water. It smelled like a campfire. I remembered all the times I wished someone would take me camping. Using a cigarette filter, she drew the liquid up into the syringe. It was cloudy and made me feel cool. I was no rock star, but I felt like one at that moment. With a rubber band wrapped around my arm, I made a fist. She pushed around on the bend of my arm, searching for a place to go in. I turned my head just as the needle slipped under my skin and deep into the vein, a tiny prick with a massive rush of goose bumps. The band around my arm came off, and the needle came out. Immediately I jumped up from the toilet seat and puked. A brown foreign liquid stared back at me from the toilet, and I felt warm all over. Warm, like lying in a field of grass with your eyes closed, letting the sun penetrate your eyelids.

Making my way back downstairs, I felt the eyes of disappointment from April and Ashley. I thought about Eric. I wondered if he thought this was cool or if he would be disappointed in me. I was out here partying on my own now, and I didn't have him as a voice of reason in my head. Although we were all in the same boat, I had taken things to a place they didn't want to be. We spent the night playing cards and chain-smoking cigarettes.

And that's where my memory ends, my memory of experimentation, my memory of life without addiction, my memory of irreversible scars.

In the following weeks, April knew something was wrong before anyone else. She saw it in my eyes. The whites were now a soft yellow. Her mother died at the hands of an aggressive liver cancer; she had seen it before. By Christmas, my skin was beginning to yellow, and depression was rolling in like an evening fog, clouding everything in front of me. The incessant itching, achy, tired joints, and an insatiable desire to sleep overwhelmed my days. It was clear something wasn't right. I was sick in an unfamiliar way. When the doctor said I tested positive for hepatitis C, I vehemently denied ever using a needle. He wanted to start an aggressive treatment immediately; my mother had reservations. She believed me when I said I hadn't used a needle. She believed me when I said this must have come from the tattoo I got on my eighteenth birthday earlier that year. And I honestly couldn't say when I contracted it. She wanted to research the side effects of the interferon treatment.

She went home and began a tireless search for all the options. According to the state of Kentucky, I was an adult. But I didn't feel like an adult in that moment. I needed my mom to tell me it would be okay and that she would find a way to make this better. But I had gone too far this time. This was something she couldn't fix. What I heard was that I was going to get sick and die. Hepatitis C doesn't necessarily work that way. It's typically a slow, progressive disease. The liver can regenerate itself. But I started writing notes to my friends, giving away my possessions. I used harder and faster than I ever had. What was the point? The damage was done. I didn't go back to the needle. Maybe out of fear. Maybe out of convenience. But I used as much and as often as I could because death felt imminent.

Word of my having hep C spread like wildfire, and everybody was afraid to get high with me, like they could catch it somehow by just being around me. Eric never made me feel that way. There's a cure now. After living with this for twenty years, I can finally breathe easier. When I went for my exam to get treated, they said mine had cleared up on its own. This only happens in 30 percent of hep C patients. Hep C and HIV rates grew exponentially from the early to mid-2000s in central Appalachia due to the prevalence of opioid addiction. As the 2010s came to a close, this region had some of the highest hep C rates in the country.

What I had was likely an acute infection, not chronic. All those years of worrying, having my own nail clippers, and making sure my razor and toothbrush weren't in contact with anyone else's, not breastfeeding Tripp—all of that was unnecessary. From the day I got my diagnosis, I thought this would kill me eventually. And I worried about it from that point on, even after I got clean. It was the part of my past I couldn't reconcile. And even though it's not transmissible anymore, I will always test positive. It will be there forever to remind me of the person I was, and if I'm not vigilant, the person I can become again.

Johnson City

2000

Eric and I caught wind of a ZZ Top show in Johnson City, Tennessee, pre–social media, and managed to find our way to the venue at nineteen. Lynyrd Skynyrd opened. It would be amazing to say I remembered that detail, but I confess I have the ticket stub. This was our first real concert. Unless you count that time I went to George Strait when I was fifteen. I went with Granny B, Vicki, and Missy, so it didn't count. I knew this time would play out differently because it was just us. This time, we were going without adult supervision. This time, we headed out on Friday afternoon with $200 worth of cocaine and pot, but no tickets. This time, we had dipped our toes into a lifestyle we weren't mature enough to understand. That lifestyle would have ramifications for years to come. My dad said we were supposed to use that $200 for a hotel room so we wouldn't have to drive back home late that night. But we didn't need to spend the night. We needed to get high.

I remember most of that trip. We listened and sang along to all our favorite ZZ Top songs. I loved it when Eric busted out his best Billy Gibbons voice. I can still see him sitting next to me with a *Tres Hombres* CD case balanced on his lap. Somewhere between Duffield and Gate City, with the steadiness of a surgeon, Eric cut out two equal white lines, rolled up a dollar bill, and passed it to me. He took the wheel from the passenger's side, keeping us on the road while I snorted my line. I guess we'd been dabbling in cocaine for a couple of years. It started showing up at parties, and we tried it. It wasn't something we did with a lot of thought or contemplation. It's hard to imagine becoming addicted to anything when you're young. We had our lives ahead of us. Teeming with possibility, we didn't see the harm. At the moment, it was perfect. We could drink more and stay up later. I wouldn't have to worry about driving back late on this trip. Cocaine made me alert and ready. In the S-10 truck mom had gotten me for graduation, the windows were black, and the music was loud. As soon as we came into range, we tuned in to WQUT, the rock station out of Johnson City. Our town didn't have a classic rock station, but sometimes when we were partying on top of the strip job back home, we could faintly pick up WQUT.

It wasn't long before we heard over the radio, "Tonight's show at the Civic Center is sold out." That should have deterred us, but I don't remember that we even cared. We were halfway to Johnson City and decided to ride it on out. No turning back now. Our only hope of getting in was finding someone in the parking lot who would sympathize with two teenagers who had just driven two and a half hours to see the greatest rock band ever. The closer we got to Johnson City, the more civilization appeared—restaurants, hotels, and big box stores. It was hard to stay focused on the road. My eyes wouldn't rest in one spot. Traffic was heavy. I kept thinking everybody in three states must be here for the show. It was probably some rush-hour situation. I always got this feeling inside when a city came into view. An excitement that puttering around back home didn't evoke. When you top that last hill, everything unfolds right before your eyes.

That place was buzzing with cars, lights, and sounds. I think about how back home in Hindman, we had just gotten our first red light. The mini-mall, with its Rite Aid and Dollar Store, made me feel like I might die if I had to spend another night parked in rows, everybody hanging out of windows. That's why you wouldn't find us lined up with the rest of the high school at the mini-mall. Instead, we would be on top of the mountain, socially lubricated, figuring things out. Even after I went away to college, I came back to Eric and the comfort of home and those nights on the mountain as often as I could.

When we pulled into the venue, it was alive with people. We were so excited and started singing "La Grange" in unison. That massive preshow party in the parking lot was like nothing we had ever seen. Some dude was setting up a tent selling knock-off band tees. People turning up beer cans left and right out of the trunks of their cars. Eric looking around, taking it all in, said, "No way we could get away with that back home. Can you imagine partying in the Dollar General parking lot?" Everybody moved with freedom, but I was anxious. I looked around, eye-ing the situation before we decided to burn a quick joint and begin our search for tickets.

We had to walk row after row of cars, asking if anybody had a spare. At some point, we realized we may have been the young-est people there. Everybody was older, closer to my dad's age. It made me wish he was with us. He was the reason we were there that day, and he is the reason music permeates every moment of our lives. My dad's life seemed to have a soundtrack. Everything he did started with booze and music. There was never a quiet moment. There was always the hum of bass in the background. J. J. Cale when he was relaxed, drinking on the porch. ZZ Top and the Rolling Stones when he was drinking in a crowd. Dire Straits when he was drinking and washing his truck. Tom Petty on Sunday when he was nursing a hangover. We've spent our whole lives watching him move, watching the way music took center stage.

We came across one ticket quickly from a guy who was cool, only making us pay face value. But we still needed another ticket, and I think Eric started freaking out at this point. I could hear it in his voice when he asked me, "What happens if we can't score another ticket?" It never crossed my mind that we might not find a way inside. It seemed to me that whenever we put our minds to something, we could make it happen. Like the uni-verse had this way of protecting us. Maybe I was optimistic to a fault. I had no reason to be. Neither of us had lived a charmed life. But the flipside of that was that we were easy to please. All we needed was any adventure that left us with a good story to tell. When we finally found a man who had an extra, he must have seen us coming. He jacked the price on us, and we didn't want to use the cash we had left to pay extra. So, Eric propositioned the guy, "How about the thirty-five dollars the ticket cost plus a couple of joints?" Most of our money was tied up in what we chose to buy before our road-trip adventures—pot, cocaine, Mountain Dew, and gas. Somehow Eric got him to agree to that and started digging for a joint.

In my mind, I was hoping this guy wasn't a cop or something. If he were, we wouldn't have to worry about where we would stay. Then, I realized that one of the joints he was about to hand this gentleman had a little blue circle drawn with an ink pen. I knew we had marked that one because it was sprinkled with coke. I panicked and grabbed it, "You can't give him that one. It has a circle." I snatched the baggie of carefully prerolled joints and found another one that wouldn't destroy this man's existence. Clearly, this guy felt a little suspicious, and I thought we had blown the whole thing. We needed that ticket if there was any chance in hell that we were both getting into the show. He was reluctant, but thank God he went through with it, and we got in line right on time.

All along the building outside the entrance, the wall was lined with pint bottles that people had to ditch before they got to security. It was a drunkard's dream. I guess drugs are a little easier to conceal because Eric made it in with our joint. Then we had to push and shove to the closest spot we could find. General admission is just a clever way of saying free-for-all, and the crowd closed in around us, jockeying for position. The whole place was buzzing as music blasted through the PA. Eric led the way and cleared the crowd. I followed close behind, trying like hell not to get separated. Then we found the perfect view in a section parallel to the stage. I still laugh thinking about that Tommy Chong look-alike who sat right beside us. Eric didn't waste any time firing up as soon as the lights went down. We were trying to play it cool, but honestly, it already smelled like someone had left a dead skunk beside the road long before we fired up. It's tricky to smoke solo at a concert. We soon learned it's common to pass the love around, except ours, which had a bonus that not everyone would enjoy.

I don't know if it was the buzz or the band, but this was unlike anything I had ever experienced. I would have sworn to you after we left there that ZZ Top had lip-synched that whole show. Everything they played was a hit, and the crowd sang along, sometimes drowning out the band. They were totally in sync. It was evident they had been playing together for thirty years. It was incredible how their movements were flawless while they were walking on treadmills. Honest to God, actual treadmills. Their beards were perfectly coiffed and stealing the show as they swayed back and forth in perfect time.

Buzzed from a laced joint and hours of our favorite music, we made our way to the merch table for a T-shirt but found awesome silver ZZ key chains instead, just like the one from the "Legs" video. We bought one each for ourselves and one for my dad. For years, we all had these on our keyrings. Years later, when Eric wrecked his car, almost killing himself, he was more worried about finding that ZZ Top key chain than being laid out on a stretcher.

As we left for home that night, we had this sense that we had conquered the world. Driving out of town, the streetlights cut the smoke in the truck cab. We couldn't stop talking about what we had just experienced. It was everything we dreamed seeing ZZ Top in concert would ever be. I laughed and gave Eric a hard time about how worked up he got because we almost didn't get in. We were destined to be at that show.

As we got further away from the hustle and bustle, the road went dark, and I didn't care about any trouble we might be in. We had checked another event off our list. We made the drive home with no issues, and as we walked in the door, Eric's mom greeted us, saying, "I knew you guys wouldn't stay."

Mandi's twenty-first birthday

Summer of Fun

2002

We deemed it the summer of fun. Kid Rock's *Cocky* was everywhere that summer, and we sang every word. It was also the first time Eric had a near-death experience. That summer, he wrecked his beloved white 1996 Camaro. The police told us if he hadn't had the T-tops off, he wouldn't have been thrown from the vehicle. Instead, he would have been trapped inside, and it would have killed him. He wasn't wearing a seat belt, a fact I remember to this day. It's the reason I don't wear mine.

At this point in our lives, the relationship had shifted. Girls became important to him, and he couldn't have his cousin tagging along. It was hard for them to understand we had been together since we were kids. I wasn't accustomed to him choosing anyone over me. For the first time in my life, I felt alone.

I spent most of that summer with Courtney, the one person my mom could trust who wouldn't let me get high. My mom had me in her version of home rehab, taking my car and supervising my visits and whereabouts.

I was home again after another failed geographical change and my third attempt at college. My last attempt took me to Western Kentucky University, four hours from home, away from my mother's watchful eye, far enough away that I knew she couldn't just show up out of the blue. Before starting Western in the fall of 2000, I spent the summer with my aunt Tina, who lived thirty miles from campus. During that time, I was able to put together a few months clean for the first time in years. I was sent to live with Tina after my hepatitis C diagnosis, two failed college attempts, and my inability to stop using left me suicidal. My mom found a note that explained who I wanted to have my belongings and why I felt like I couldn't go on. Leaving school again and going to live with Tina seemed like a failure at the time. However, it likely saved my life. I spent the summer by the pool, reading and making Mod Podge art. I felt like my authentic self again, and it renewed my spirit.

But when I stepped onto that college campus, no matter how good my intentions were, it wasn't long before I found my people. Off and running again. My stint at Pikeville College taught me that, at the very least, I needed to attend class. That was half the battle of getting through school. So, I did it in my own fucked-up way. I bought cigarettes; dumped the tobacco, replacing it with finely ground pot; packed it in; and smoked on my walk to class. I'm not sure who I thought I was fooling. I'd pass groups walking together, laughing, and telling tales. I envied those people. I tried to understand why I couldn't have that. Why couldn't I drink on Saturday nights and take care of business on Monday mornings? Make friends and laugh about our weekends on the way to class? Instead, I spent most of my time alone and wanted to be high all the time. There was never a cutoff point. This made an eight-in-the-morning philosophy class interesting, and apparently, I hadn't learned enough not to schedule an eight o'clock class.

My roommate lived with her boyfriend off campus except when her mom visited, which was the perfect arrangement for both of us. She was never interested in forming a friendship. I could only make friends with people I could get high with. All other relationships proved to be a challenge. Crippling shyness and insecurities made it hard to forge any genuine bonds. Whatever cash my mom was sending was never enough. I couldn't fuel my habit and eat. I couldn't fuel my habit and afford anything, for that matter. I decided to work as a night security guard at a factory in town.

I thought this was the perfect solution. It wouldn't interfere with my classes, and I could do all my homework while I sat around all night. It would be perfect; I wouldn't have to deal with any people, and I would be making money. That's not exactly how it turned out. I would sneak outside and smoke pot most of my shift if I could stay awake. I'd get high and go through everyone's desks. I wasn't looking to steal as much as killing time. Observing people's lives, college diplomas, family photos, and favorite pens. It all seemed like a world out of reach, one I wasn't sure I would ever fit into.

It just so happened that the guy that owned the company loved to smoke crack and take pain meds, a fact I didn't know until a few weeks in. He ran the business out of his home office. An average ranch style tucked away in a quiet neighborhood, homes with kids playing in the yard, people walking dogs, and minivans in the driveway—a stark contrast to what was going on behind his four walls. We'd sit around and chat when I went to pick up my checks on Fridays. It didn't take long for those chats to turn into using. Misery loves company, and it must have been tattooed on my face. This was a recipe for disaster. This guy was at least twenty years older than me, maybe. I can't be sure. At the ripe age of nineteen, everyone seems old, I guess. His trust in me grew in time, and we'd make trips to Nashville to score crack, and we'd smoke it on the drive back to Bowling Green. He had prescriptions that he was willing to share. Even so, there were times when I broke into his house and took them. It's clear now how dangerous this situation was and how lucky I am that he didn't take advantage of me. This was new territory for me; I had to do things I had never done before to get high. He was a stranger to me, and I was breaking into his house. I wasn't protected by my small town anymore. I couldn't charge dope here. No one cared if I was dope-sick. I tried to remedy that by working, but there was never enough money or drugs.

That semester was a lot of the same. I was working a ridiculous shift trying to keep my head above water in all my classes and spending a lot of time finding dope and getting high. No football games or frat parties. No late-night study groups in the library. No diploma to hang on the wall of my future office. I went into that semester on academic probation, so I didn't have a large margin for error. College number three: fail.

I had no way of knowing what I was coming home to. Over the past year and a half, I'd had no communication with my friends in eastern Kentucky. OxyContin was everywhere. People I had known my whole life who would never have considered taking drugs were now fully addicted. By the summer of 2002, the effects of Purdue Pharma's aggressive marketing campaign were evident all over eastern Kentucky. In a region plagued by high cancer rates and chronic pain due to the physical demands of coal industry work, the numbers for non-OxyContin opioid prescriptions were 2.5 to 5.0 percent higher than the national average. This was how Purdue Pharma decided where to spend its marketing dollars. During this time, pain became a vital sign, and there were trends to liberate the prescribing of opioids to treat general pain. Purdue Pharma targeted physicians with high opioid prescribing rates and courted them like it was Saturday night. They implemented a patient starter coupon program for free limited prescriptions up to a thirty-day supply. If that doesn't reek of a corporate attempt to get people hooked, I don't know what does. This was a tactic that street dealers used for years. But when you put on a suit and it comes from a pharmacy, people are slower to catch on. By the time the program ended, thirty-four thousand coupons had been redeemed.

Applebee's had just opened in Hazard, becoming a hot drinking spot. I had been using pretty heavily up to this point. My mom's in-home treatment technique that summer took me back to a time when partying was innocent and fun, riding around with Courtney in her Honda, singing our assigned parts to "Picture." It was carefree, without the burden of trying to score dope every day. Granted, we spent a lot of time drunk that summer, but that was before I fully understood addiction and all its ramifications—the fact that addicts don't meet a substance they don't love.

That same summer, I was weaning myself off Paxil, an antidepressant I had been on for a few years. It was the first time I had received treatment for depression, something that had plagued me since puberty—and something I still battle today. I know depression came first, and I think now that this may be the source of my using. It's almost impossible to pinpoint the moment when everything shifted. When it became a have-to thing and not a choice. It is gradual and hard to define. The nature of these types of drugs changes brain chemistry. That, coupled with withdrawal from opiates, left me on the floor of the bathroom with excruciating headaches and sparks in my brain. I was acutely aware of every synapse that fired.

I was at Courtney's the night Eric wrecked his car. My mom came to tell me in the middle of the night. It was the first time I grappled with the idea that I might have to live without him, this notion that we are mortal and that one of us wouldn't make it out of this alive.

When we arrived at the hospital, I learned that Eric and his friend Tim had wrecked the Camaro in a straight stretch right before Jones Fork Mountain. I know he was pushing it to its limits, testing it out, and showing it off. He was so proud of that car. Eric and Tim were both in critical condition, and I will never forget how Eric looked in that hospital bed. Thinking you can be thrown from a vehicle and live is mind-boggling. They both denied driving to the cops. They never figured out who was driving, so no one was charged. Always clever, always careful. That's one way we differed. I was all-in for everything. No thought to consequence, no regard for tomorrow. I always had Eric to check my decision-making at a time when my decision-making wasn't that strong. We were a long way from swimming out too far in the pond—a long way from the days when I protected him. Now I needed someone to ensure I wasn't over my head.

Euclid Avenue

2003

When Jake picked us up, he was already high. He had been high, in fact, for days and hadn't slept in that time. I recognized the dark circles. I saw how his whole body seemed to vibrate. Despite being addicted, he was strikingly handsome. Piercing blue eyes that became more pronounced as his pupils got smaller. Clean cut, with his square jaw freshly shaven, hanging on to his conservative roots. His white undershirt fit tightly around his arms and chest. He kept himself fit.

I was accustomed to searching for drugs in a new town. After a couple of unsuccessful attempts at geographical change and continuing to rack up failures after so many attempts to outrun my addiction and me, I found myself in Lexington. My boyfriend, Grant, and I had only been in Lexington for a few days when we heard that Jake lived here too. We knew Jake from back home, so that's when we knew we had our connection. It's always funny to me how addicts spot each other. It's like we wear signs announcing that life would be more fun if we all ganged up in the bathroom for some blow. Every town I found myself in, I managed to see the signs, neon and flashing, no matter how hard I tried not to—leaving a path of destruction from one end of the state to the other.

Jake had just sold a motorcycle, and at some point, I guess he was tired of talking to himself all night. With a pocket full of motorcycle money, he decided to get us high, and that's all I needed to know. Almost immediately, his rambling talking and his choice of music annoyed me. Linkin Park's "Numb" blared from the stereo, and he had to scream over it to be heard. I was already agitated because I hadn't gotten high that day, and this made it worse. Fellow junkie friends often forget that we're not all on the same plane at any given time.

Although I was not a fan of Linkin Park, I could see how Jake related to this song. He was always caught up in trying to follow the path of his career-politician father. Lines of a song that could have applied to any of us. But when he sang them, I felt the weight of his burden.

We made our way out of the grit of downtown and away from the rows of student housing to Jake's upscale suburban neighborhood. Mapped-out blocks with sidewalks and manicured lawns. I'm pretty sure it was his family's second home.

I lived with Grant and two other people in a two-bedroom apartment. Jake's place was tidy and well-furnished, different from the places where I had smoked crack. He pulled out a marble-size rock from the watch pocket of his jeans. It looked dingy and delicious. I already dreaded the need for more—the deep, uncomfortable longing for relief, all my senses pulsating on edge. It wouldn't stop me from going down this well-traveled road; it never had, and as far as I could tell, it never would. So, when desire presented itself, I fed it.

They let me take the first hit from a long glass test tube–like cylinder. I had seen these glass tubes before by the cash register at all-night truck stops. Affectionately marketed as a "love rose," it's nothing more than a silk flower encased in a glass tube and offered in a rainbow of colors. At the time, I tried to imagine a trucker picking one up to take home to his wife after days on the road. But there at Jake's apartment in the good part of Lexington, I shoved a piece of Chore Boy in one end to act as a screen. The key, I had learned, is to apply heat slowly, letting it melt and burn at an even temperature without cracking the glass. Slowing down during the process would be more of a challenge as the night went on.

I allowed the tube to fill with smoke and took a long hard drag, holding it deep in my lungs until I was out of breath. The smoke was smooth and smelled like acetone. It reminded me of my mom, of how she would remove and reapply her nail polish before going out at night. Immediately my heart raced like I was in love, excited about the thought of being close to another. A lump in my throat made it hard to speak or swallow. The ringing in my ears was deafening. Their lips were moving, but I couldn't hear what they were saying. Sweat dripped down my face, and my palms were clammy. I lay down because the room was going black in the corners of my eyes. I felt like I might pass out. I wasn't in this space anymore, although I could feel the cool leather of the couch on my bare legs, and I could see my reflection on the polished hardwood floors.

But I was somewhere else, a place where all the pain had been taken away, and there were no more fears or insecurities. I worried it was too much and that my heart might explode. I checked the pulse in my neck and counted the beats. I wondered how many beats would signal a heart attack. We passed the tube back and forth, chasing that jolt of lightning. It was Jake's money, so it was his crack. He was in control of the frequency. But that's the problem with crack. No amount is enough, and the time between hits is too long. We paced around his suburban fortress, prolonging the trips to the love rose.

The finishes in the house were nice, but the space was sparsely furnished. The living room was empty, aside from an overstuffed couch and a huge television. I can imagine what this house would be with its three-bedroom/two-bath layout. A husband and wife, two kids, and a dog in the large backyard. Nights grilling on the deck that extended past the glass double doors off the kitchen. I focused on a framed photo hanging over the couch of the Lexington skyline, dipped in blue Maker's Mark wax. At the bottom, it read, "Mark of a Great Town." It was hard for me to believe it. The Lexington I knew didn't seem so great.

At the end of the night, the euphoria was gone. That little ball left us looking around the room for a crumb we might have dropped, pushing the steel wool back and forth through the glass tube with the hope of one more hit.

And there it was. The thing I dreaded—the longing for something more. For something. Something that would take me away from feeling like a failure and not living up to my potential. A break from the relentless grind of drug addiction. Something that would take away those feelings of never finding a place where I belong. Something that would take me to a place in my mind where I didn't care about finding someone to love me. Something to fill the hole and fix me even for a brief moment.

Bust It Up

2003

My pulse was racing. There was a lump in my throat. I could hardly swallow. My mouth was dry. As I snuck up the steps, I was careful not to step on the boards I knew would creak. I had these steps memorized. I knew every groove, crevice, and soft spot that gave way to a moaning sound when it was stepped on. When I reached the landing, the morning light coming through the windows was blinding.

I was here in my childhood bedroom to clean out the pockets of two of my most beloved friends: Eric and Sara, my childhood friend. Sara moved away when we were thirteen. I went to college in her new hometown. We reconnected as though no time had passed. That's the beauty of an old friend. We were back home for the weekend, house-sitting for my mom. The pain that engulfed me was my constant motivation, driving this relentless need for relief.

My bedroom looked precisely how I left it. Right in the center of my bed, there were body parts on display that I shouldn't be privy to. I could tell the two of them slept together. But we were all grown, right? That was not my concern at that point. I needed money for a fix, and this was the obvious opportunity that day. Clothes were in piles on the floor. Sara's jeans were just within reach. I swiped a fifty, careful not to wake anyone.

The phone calls began. You can't say why you're really calling.

"Ya'll doing anything today?"

"Yeah, ride up."

They knew why I was calling. There was no need for a conversation. It was like calling the master of your destiny. It was something like a lifeline. Getting a pill wasn't as easy as ordering a cheeseburger. I couldn't just decide I wanted one, then drive by and pick it up. There was always a game: sit around and make nice with your dealer, share with your dealer, or wait around for your dealer until he was back from some far-off state where pill mills were generous. It was commonplace for dealers and doers alike to head out for all-day trips to Dayton, Ohio, or someplace in Florida. In small towns like ours, doctors were subject to having their practices completely shut down due to the high volume of narcotics being prescribed. Away from eastern Kentucky, it was easier to conceal, I suppose. People poured into those places in droves every month to maintain a prescription.

I could never just be. The anticipation, the cramping in the stomach, all while on the verge of tears—this was all a part of the game. And heaven forbid, my connection was just out of pills altogether, and I had to involve someone else in this show. I was not considering cutting anybody in today. I needed all forty milligrams.

OxyContin came in twenty-, forty-, and eighty-milligram pills. In the beginning, it might be that a couple of us would split a twenty. Then a forty. My tolerance for OxyContin built up quickly. I needed a higher dose to get high. Then I needed a higher dose to get well. Soon none of us wanted to share. OxyContin was still a dollar a milligram, so most of the time, sharing was a necessity. But this day, there were no boyfriends to consider and no friends who would beg for a line in exchange for their connection. No family members whose drug addiction I catered to as if it were my own. All manner of decency was spared. And so, the guilt and shame crept in. I stole the money, and I was selfish, too. Just another layer to cover up. The prescription does say to take for pain as needed, and I was so familiar with the pain.

My dealer's house was a second home. I played with his kids and caught up with his wife. None of this felt out of line to me.

It reminded me of weekends with my family. It felt normal for kids to be around. They offered me a bologna sandwich. It was apparent that I hadn't been eating regularly. Even though I was embarrassed, I took the sandwich. Pain pills are expensive, and there was never any money left. I gave him the fifty, and he went off into his bedroom while I nervously sat on their couch and waited. Here, I felt at home and accepted. I didn't have to pretend I was something I wasn't. I felt more at home here than I did with my own family.

When you score, it's like Christmas. The anticipation of that moment, the moment when you know everything will be okay, leaves you giddy with excitement. Already, the pain begins to subside. He returned after an eternity, and something inside me settled. I asked them to use the plate and straw they kept tucked under their couch. OxyContin was meant to be a time-released medication that could be taken once daily for chronic pain. Someone soon realized that if the outside coating was removed, all the ingredients could be administered immediately. This was the design flaw I took advantage of.

Placing the pill inside my mouth, I dissolved the coating; I wiped it off using my shirt. It left a yellow stain—evidence that the lies couldn't cover up. Like the night me and Eric peeled apples with Dovie and thought she couldn't smell alcohol on us. Or all those cigarettes we'd sneak, thinking no one could smell the smoke. But when it comes to things like these, people choose what they want to see. Placing the pill on the plate, I put a dollar bill over the top, bust it up, and smooth it out with a pop lid. I cut a nice manageable line and snorted it up my nose. Immediately, I was in a world of possibilities, flooded with boundless energy and no fears. All the social pressures and uncertainty lifted. I was exactly who I wanted to be with no reservations. I liken this to waiting in line for a roller coaster: hours of anticipation and achy legs for a three-minute rush.

But for a brief moment, every day, I was balanced. I would find a job and get out on my own, out from under my mother's watchful eye. I would finish that degree I had started a hundred times. I would get clean once and for all. This would be it. I didn't need drugs; I wasn't like everybody else that cycled in and out of here. I realized my potential. They were just junkies. But in the end, every day would bring the same pain, the same guilt and shame that drove my drug addiction forward. I would chase that relief from myself for as long as I could. I longed for the day when I could achieve some contentment without using chemicals. To move through the world as others do.

Lethal Combination

2004

The line between nothingness and death is thin. It is figuring out how much to take to find a magical state of equilibrium. My goal was to find a state of being so far away from living that my only function left was breath. Complete numbness of the body and mind, a shutdown of all the parts of my brain that react and obsess over the outside world. The anxiety and obligations quieted as the brain was flooded with feel-good chemicals.

Most addicts feel invincible, I guess, or think they know how much they can use to walk this tightrope. Or maybe they don't care. I know I didn't. Prescription pain meds are different from street drugs because you know what you're getting. When I was using, you did. I knew exactly how much I needed to keep from getting dope-sick, and I knew exactly how much I needed to get high. Tolerance for pain meds grows quickly; the longer you use, the more it takes to fend off dope-sickness, meaning the more it takes to get high. Sometimes I'd have to mix drugs to get the desired effect. I mixed alcohol and pot, but mostly I mixed a combination of pills. This was brought on because of the cost of OxyContin. At a price tag of over a dollar a milligram, that runs into a lot of money every day, which turns into a lot of shady shit to get that money every day. If you need an OC-80 to keep from getting sick, that's $100 a day. And that's only to keep from being sick. That's before you get high. You can see how quickly this can add up. Especially with a growing tolerance, the need for more continues to increase. I found combinations of drugs that accelerated the high or made it cheaper. Ironically, doctors would prescribe opiates and benzodiazepines together, which is a great combination. My reasoning and the doctors' reasoning are probably different. But this combination is also lethal—especially methadone and Xanax.

That's what happened to Eric. A night of methadone and Xanax. That was around 2004, when he was living with his mom. I was living with Grant in the house I grew up in after my mom had had enough and moved out and rented an apartment on her own in a neighboring town. That's how bad I was at the time; she didn't even try to kick *me* out. She packed her stuff and left.

It was a dark time. Grant and I barely made ends meet. We had one car and one job between the two of us, which meant I stayed home most days, dope-sick and waiting. Grant was working underground for a mining company. Lots of men I knew worked underground to support their habit. It's ironic that a job that breaks you down physically was also a means of support for a pain pill habit. It was easy for men. They could get a job like this that paid a decent wage and have the respect of the community. They were shoveling coal all day, buried in a space they couldn't stand up in. The options women had to support their addictions weren't respectable.

"Eric's overdosed, and they are taking him to Hazard. He's alive, but it ain't good. I'm not working today. I'm on my way to get you," Grant said.

I hung up the phone and waited for Grant.

We heard Eric died in the ambulance. This was before Narcan. When we got to the hospital, the lobby was already full. All our family and some of the people we regularly got high with. It was an uncomfortable group of people to be around—like the two parts of my life were sitting in a room together. These were not people who typically converged, but at that moment, the addicts were still concerned with getting high. This is what I'm trying to describe—the inability to feel the intensity of that moment. Even though Eric was lying there, dying from taking too much, we were all trying to find a way to sneak out to the parking lot to snort a pill. The insanity of addiction is unparalleled.

Mom showed up during all this chaos, stalking me like prey. The likelihood of me going out to the parking lot unnoticed to get a fix was damn near impossible. She relives this day a lot; nonaddicts rarely see the insanity in action. She likes returning to that waiting room when Eric's mom said, "I told him not to mix those two together." My mom was appalled that this was her response to what had happened. My mom loved Eric so much and always wished his circumstances had been different. She knew it would be hard for him to get clean like this.

There was a clear divide in that waiting room between the people who struggled with addiction and those who did not. Addicts talk too much. They say dumb shit to fill the void. I think it may be a coping skill or a tactic to try to fool everyone around them that they're not high—which never works, by the way.

Eventually, I had to do it. I had to go in and see him. It's not that I didn't want to. It's that I didn't know how to. I'd gotten pretty good at avoiding life, but I couldn't avoid this. He was in the ICU, but it was just a more extensive space, partitioned by a curtain. It smelled sterile and beeped, as hospitals do. The hospital only permitted one visitor at a time. When I walked into the room, they had him on his belly with his head turned to one side and a long tube coming out of his mouth. It was doing all the breathing.

He didn't have his own breath.

I'd never seen anyone on their belly in a hospital before. So there we were, alone in this room, me not knowing if he would live or die, wishing I was a little higher because this was breaking my heart. We were never ones for chats about feelings. We never hugged or said we loved each other. Hell, we saw each other every day. I knew he loved me, and he knew I loved him. Nobody was going anywhere. There was no need for all that. But here we were, in a situation where he very well might be leaving, and I wasn't sure how to respond. He was unconscious, but I took his hand and talked to him. It felt weird and pointless at the time, and I'm not sure I would have done that for anybody else. I remember how rough his hand felt. That was a detail I didn't know. I wondered if he could hear me as the ventilator sucked in and out like lungs taking a breath. The sound of each compression filled the room.

"There is no way I can do this on my own. I love you. Please don't leave me here alone." And as I spoke, tears started streaming down his face. Could he hear me, or was this a trauma response to being on a ventilator?

We never talked about it.

He didn't die that time. Eventually, he was released. I hated that he had to go home to the same bedroom he got high in. The same bedroom the paramedics found him in. Where his lips turned blue and his respiratory rate decreased, the line between nothingness and death getting thinner and thinner. I still can't believe they didn't offer him any counseling or treatment options. Instead, they just slapped him on the ass and sent him on his way—no follow-up appointments or hospital surveys asking about his stay. Although addiction is classified as a disease, this is a good example of how it's not treated like other diseases. People think addiction is self-inflicted.

When he called to talk about his release, I could tell he was nervous about being back home. His house was always full of action and people coming in and out. For most of my life, I had envied his situation. I was alone so often. I would have loved all that activity. But he never got a break. Somebody was always getting him high. And that's a situation to envy until you don't want to get high anymore.

He was scared and, for the first time, considered a life of something more. But he had no support. Where would he even start? People cannot recover in isolation, which would have been his only choice at this point, surrounded by others who got high. I could tell he was foggy. He was quiet and had a faraway look in his eyes. I worried that some critical part of his brain had been damaged due to lack of oxygen. I worried that he would never fully recover.

There is no prognosis when you overdose. Life is the prognosis. I wanted him to come live with me. Grant and I lived in the cabin my parents lived in when they married. I knew he wouldn't commit to a permanent move, but I thought it might be a nice option until he could figure out what was next. Although Grant and I were far from clean, we lived in the head of a holler and didn't get many visitors. If we didn't use in front of him, I thought his chances of getting a pill were slim.

He agreed to come stay with us for a while. He complained to me about a ringing in his ears, which was almost unbearable for him. He worried he would have to live with it forever. Eric and I sat around smoking and drinking during the day while Grant went to work. We still only had one car between the three of us. We had an Alice in Chains MTV-unplugged DVD that we sat and watched endlessly. I'd bought each of us a copy one year for Christmas. It was our favorite album, and we loved analyzing Layne Staley's performance.

During this time, Purdue Pharma started an aggressive anti-story marketing campaign. They attempted to change the narrative surrounding OxyContin, using medical professionals paid mainly by Purdue directly or through donations to their respective corporations. They were claiming that addicts, not the medication, were the problem. They said that if OxyContin was taken as prescribed, it was a safe and effective means to treat long-term pain. I know from experience this isn't true. It has been proven that anyone who takes oxycodone for a prolonged period risks addiction.

Purdue played on the public's sympathies, making it look like pain patients were paying the price for closely monitored prescriptions. They still insisted that OxyContin had a less than 1 percent addiction rate if taken as prescribed. Purdue Pharma attempted to play the victim, trying to convince whomever was listening that their product had been demonized. It's funny to me that in the wave of OxyContin's release, pain became a problem that suddenly needed to be treated, with pain clinics popping up everywhere, and people who were newly addicted to opioids traveled miles away to get their hands on OxyContin. Appalachians drove as far as Florida on what was dubbed the OxyContin Express to access prescriptions that weren't being monitored in a tracking system. As prevalent as OxyContin was, it still had considerable consequences for those who couldn't get a prescription. I was constantly chasing the high I found from OCs. Most of us were, even if this meant taking what we knew was a lethal combination.

In those moments, I wished I had the resources to get both Eric and me out of there. I dreamed of leaving behind all this addiction and sickness, the same everyday shit *Groundhog Day* situation, and starting over somewhere new. But there was no magical place to start over. You must start from where you're at, which seemed like the most impossible task. But for a moment in those couple of weeks, getting stoned and watching TV, eating crap dairy bar food, we got a break from the grind. And I had Eric back. But, of course, it wouldn't last. Eventually, we would retreat to our corners, surviving every day the best way we knew how. And soon everybody forgot that he'd almost died. We got comfortable again. We stopped wearing our seat belts.

ACCEPTANCE
2005–2013

Before There Was Treatment

2005

I don't have the words to describe what it feels like to crave a chemical down to your core. The best comparison I can find is a cliché—a fish out of water. But imagine actually being a fish out of water—needing one thing to survive.

On New Year's Eve 2005, I stepped out into the brisk cold night and smoked a cigarette alone on the porch. My boyfriend, Grant, and I were at a party. We were broke and desperate. There was alcohol, but that never seemed to satisfy the hunger. There was no hope of copping the buzz I needed that night. We had exhausted all our resources.

I knew something had to change. I couldn't continue living in the prison substance use kept me in. I asked God, the same God I struggled with then and now, to get me out of this situation. I said it out loud to whomever was listening. I could see my breath. I knew my words were genuine. That night, I made a promise to God that if he got me out of this mess and got me to the other side of addiction, I would never use again.

The following day, I woke up and hit the ground running, like I had all the mornings before. Where's the dope? Where's the money coming from? I continued to live that life for another three and a half months. I had quickly forgotten the deal I made with God—but whomever was listening failed to ignore the agreement with me. Something happened in April that changed the course of my life.

Grant and I still only had one car, so once he left for work, I was stuck at home until he returned. Most days, that meant I was dope-sick, rationing cigarettes, and trying to make a meal out of nothing. A friend who was also in active addiction visited me. She came to my rescue that morning in more ways than one.

After she blessed me with a biscuit, a cigarette, and a pill, she made a decision that pissed me off *and* set me free. She left that day and went straight to where my mom worked. She told her I needed help and needed it fast. That afternoon played out like something from the television show *Intervention*. My mom showed up and laid out an ultimatum. I knew I would be homeless, carless, and hopeless without her. If I chose drugs at that very moment, it's possible that I wouldn't have lived to tell the tale. The following day, I went to detox.

Before I went into rehab, there was detox. Before I could get clean, I had to *be* clean. I had tried to get into treatment before, and they told me I didn't use enough and that my suicidal thoughts weren't real enough because I didn't have a plan. This was after I had flunked out of three colleges and burned bridges in every town I'd lived in. Eric and I weren't hanging out much then, but I guess he knew I was stealing to get high, and I stayed high all the time. I was sick when I didn't have dope, couldn't hold down a job, and couldn't go to school. I couldn't believe a professional looked me in the eye and told me I didn't qualify for inpatient services.

Can you imagine turning someone suffering from an active addiction loose when they were willing to give up drugs? I could go through their outpatient program, they said, which required daily meetings two hours from home. If I was free, I was using, meeting or no meeting. I felt like I needed to be separated from the world at a time like this.

When I didn't qualify for inpatient care and knew I couldn't manage meetings two hours away, I started seeing an outpatient drug and alcohol counselor at a mental health facility close to home. Most people were there to meet the requirements for a recent DUI or drug charge. I guess it was rare for someone to seek help on their own without some legal repercussions. And truthfully, I was there partly to get Mom off my back. The failed attempt at rehab brought many of my secrets to the surface, and she was rightfully concerned about my use. I lied and told her I wanted to stop using drugs and that I would try to do it on my own. Maybe it wasn't a total lie. Somewhere deep inside, I did want to stop. Nobody wants to live that way. But wanting to and doing are two different things. I thought my only options at that point were overdose or suicide.

I wish there was a magic cure for the disease of addiction. It's not like other diseases. You don't receive a diagnosis and then begin treatment. It's a lifelong battle, and it takes years to uncover all the layers. Everybody's always looking for someone or something to blame—something concrete. It's not easy, and for some, that opportunity never comes. Cycles of jails and institutions prevent addicts from making actual breakthroughs. If you're lucky, you can string together some time in recovery and start to unpack all the nuances of your behavior. And I do consider myself lucky.

I saw a counselor weekly and took classes at the community college. My outward appearance would lead one to believe I was making a real effort to turn things around. But addicts lie. My therapy appointments and classes gave me an excuse to leave the house. Living with my mom at the time, I was under close observation. She kept me on a short leash and monitored my whereabouts closely.

Loved ones of those who suffer from addiction get themselves into a codependent trap. The people closest to you feel like they have the power to exert control over the situation and can somehow manipulate the outcome. But no one can stop an addict from using until they're ready. Not their kids, their parents, or the legal system. In some situations, you can love someone to death by enabling them and making their drug use easy or more comfortable without allowing any natural consequences for their actions. It sets a person up to disappoint everyone around them, perpetuating the never-ending cycle of guilt and shame.

Every week, I used therapy as an opportunity to escape my house to get high. I would stop by Eric's house on the way and joke about how I had to talk about feelings. I would talk a lot of shit during those appointments and probably thought I was convincing. Maybe I was. I didn't blame the system or my parents. I was painfully self-aware and felt I knew many reasons why I got high. But I wasn't able to face it all, evidenced by the fact that I went to months of therapy high as hell. I can't recall one conversation we had during those sessions.

I knew I was at the end of the road and needed help soon. I couldn't be out in the real world for another day. I was suicidal, and I began to realize I had a plan I had been executing for ten years, slowly, one day at a time. From the minute I started using drugs and alcohol daily, I wanted to die. Not on a conscious level, but somewhere inside, I knew I didn't care what the outcome of my actions was. I never told anyone, but the first time I thought of suicide, I was fifteen. That time, I did have a plan. I would go into the woods up on Ropeworks and shoot myself with a gun no one around me owned, thank God.

When I was presented with the opportunity to go to detox, I lied again for a different reason. I lied to get the help I needed. I lied so that I could stop dying. I exaggerated how much I was using, hoping they would let me in. This new life required me to be uncomfortably honest in everything I had done with a lie.

From that day when I was fifteen, imagining suicide, I found other ways to escape that pain. I wasn't brave enough to take my own life, but if I used enough or drove fucked up enough, maybe something would happen, and that wouldn't be my fault. That wouldn't disappoint everyone. I never wanted to disappoint anyone.

When I walked into detox, I told them I was using double what I was. I was admitted immediately. Mom left me there with a cold goodbye. My vital signs were measured daily. I told them I didn't want methadone. I had been getting high off methadone, so I didn't understand how that could be effective. I shared a room with a woman in her sixties who became addicted to OxyContin after back surgery. She told me she had never as much as smoked a cigarette, and she couldn't believe she wound up here. This was a time when doctors still believed in OxyContin. Purdue Pharma propagated the idea that only people abusing OxyContin became addicted. That this was somehow a moral issue. OxyContin was marketed as safe and effective when taken as directed. But here, this woman had become just as addicted as I was. Neither one of us was at fault for the circumstances we found ourselves in. Some people might argue that point. But I know that OxyContin was marketed and distributed in a way that made it accessible to anyone and everyone who needed or wanted it, regardless of the nature of their pain.

There was a TV room with a mini fridge with an endless supply of peanut-butter-and-jelly sandwiches and little juice cups with foil lids and ice cream with wooden sticks to eat it with. Uncomfortable seats like in a doctor's office waiting room. A coffee machine that dripped caffeine all hours of the day and night. There was a smoking room—all glass, like an observation tank, except you couldn't observe anything for the smoke that lingered on the inside, lingered on my clothes and in the air like so many stale, sad rooms before. People spent a lot of time in there, me included, smoking USA Golds. On the way to drop me off, when I asked the man behind the counter at the gas station for Marlboros, my mom had said, "No, she'll take the USA Golds."

That may have been the only thing she said the whole way there. She didn't want to take me. She'd had enough of me. We rode in silence the entire way. Her last jab at me came in the form of these cheap cigarettes.

The rec room/cafeteria had a ping-pong table, pool table, and some lunchroom tables. I didn't feel much like any kind of table in the days that followed. There was a medication window where we'd go in the morning and before bed at night for something to help us sleep and keep us from shitting all day. And that's what I did. I slept and stayed on the toilet for at least two days. I felt like I hadn't slept in years.

But to be compliant, I had to go to group and eat—both things I detested, given my need to shit and sleep. We had access to a pay phone, but I didn't have anyone who wanted to talk to me except my aunt Tina, who told me everything would be okay. And I believed her.

They kept me for five days because that's what the insurance allowed, not because I was ready to go. Not because I didn't want to kill myself anymore. Not because I was cured. I walked up to the window every night, getting my paper cup of pills and sticking out my tongue. I was starting to feel like maybe I could shoot a game of pool, and I was beginning to enjoy those peanut-butter-and-jelly sandwiches in the TV room. I still couldn't have strings in my shoes or my hoodies. But I was starting to read again. I was reading a book called *The Basic Text* that they gave me when I checked in. It was the bible for Narcotics Anonymous. It's not what I wanted to read, but it's all I had. I had no idea how that book would change my life. My blood pressure was out of control. My body was rejecting this new way of life.

"I'm Mandi, and I'm an addict," I had to say before speaking in group. When I prepared to leave, my counselor printed off a meeting schedule for me. Mom picked me up. I don't think she was thrilled with this arrangement. Five days wasn't enough time to forgive and forget. She had been down this road with me enough to know the chances I wouldn't get high again immediately were slim. But there was no one else to take me home, and the alternative was being on the streets. I was fortunate enough to begin my recovery journey in Hazard.

I moved in with Mom when I got out of detox instead of going back to Hales Branch. Hazard had at least one meeting a night and a couple of lunch meetings weekly. She drove me straight to an NA meeting from detox. I was scared and didn't want to go alone. She went in and sat beside me.

It was a meeting in the old courthouse. I was surprised I didn't recognize anyone out of the twenty or thirty people there. I mostly just sat quietly and listened that first night. I had to wait two weeks before I could get in anywhere long-term. In the meantime, I attended at least one meeting daily because that was suggested while I was in detox. The process of finding residential treatment left me feeling frustrated and hopeless. There weren't enough facilities in the region to accommodate the growing number of people with opioid problems. If I had been pregnant and on the needle, I would have moved to the top of the list; otherwise, I had to wait. If I had gone to the homeless shelter, there would be a meeting every day and somewhere to sleep, but you had to be out of the building at all other times, presumably on the street. Even my mom, with her tough love tactics, wasn't ready for that.

I began to chase recovery in the same manner I chased dope. The irony of the situation is that I went back to see the same therapist after I got out of treatment. I discovered that drugs weren't my problem after I stopped using them. Mental illness lies at the core of my disease. I was seeing her and attending twelve-step meetings. If there was an avenue for information, I wanted it. I wanted to know everything about addiction, the science behind it, the long-term effects of brain chemistry, and how others had managed to stop compulsive comfort-seeking. I had to have all the information. I thought this would prevent a relapse. Relapsing would make me unlovable. I would be a disappointment. I wanted to be the best-recovering addict. I wanted to do it perfectly. Addiction doesn't stop when the drugs are taken away.

Next Step

2005

I awoke to bugs working their way out from under my skin. I had to get up and undress before I found it was just my imagination. My body ached for drugs on a molecular level. It felt like something wasn't wired up right inside of me. This is what I had become. I was sharing a room with a stranger, two twin beds pushed against the wall, a chest of drawers tucked neatly between them. Back to cold tile floors, scratchy sterile sheets, fluorescent lights, and a flat pillow. This building used to be an office complex but was converted into a fourteen-day treatment facility.

This wasn't a dorm room. Fourteen days. Who can kick dope in fourteen days? This was just the tip of the iceberg for the barrage of treatment facilities that flooded the region in the coming years, and it still wouldn't be enough for the onslaught of people desperate for a reprieve from the sorrows of everyday life. I found myself here after a pseudo-intervention of friends and family. Any of my friends who escaped OxyContin's grips were fortunate. Eric hadn't escaped.

I woke before daylight every morning to clean my room and make my bed. This was recovery on the most basic level. I was responsible for helping keep the bathroom clean. Slick tan tile with grout stained beyond cleaning, the faint smell of urine and Clorox, wet hairs stuck all around. "They should have maintenance for this," I thought. I was here to get off drugs, not clean bathrooms. At least, I hoped that's what would happen. I was sure I wanted to stop using drugs, but I knew nothing about living without them. I also had to keep the common area clean—a couple of mismatched couches donated by some upstanding citizens, and an old floor-model TV. The last time I saw something like it was Saturday morning cartoons and Rainbow Brite cereal.

I sure didn't feel like cereal and cartoons. We cooked as a team, preparing breakfast for everyone and cleaning up afterward. It was the most unselfish thing I had done in months. I don't recall making breakfast for myself while I was high, let alone for a whole group. I was so tired, my body craved sleep like it craved pills. The rest I had been getting here couldn't make up for the last seven years I'd spent high or dope-sick.

This was not my idea of recovering. I pictured a tropical climate with naps and group outings. Someplace named after rock stars. During our group sessions, the counselors turned the lights out and showed us a movie about people who had survived the perils of addiction and turned their lives around, and we could, too, if only we were willing to surrender the only coping skill we had ever known. I could not fathom never being able to escape my mind again. Heaven forbid I gave in to my body's need for sleep and slowly closed my eyes. If I did, they would send me to my room to write about why I felt sleeping was a better choice than saving my life. There were times when I highly considered taking that writing punishment for fifteen minutes of sleep.

We would have free time in the common area or outside between group and individual therapy sessions. A couple of worn-out picnic tables with peeling redwood stain and a basketball hoop with no net, barely hanging on to the pole. God, how I used to love the game of basketball. I remember Papaw playing with me for hours in our front yard, teaching me proper form. Teaching me to step on the opponent's toes when you rebound. Most of my childhood was on a court, typically basketball or tennis, pleasing everyone around me with my athletic skill and academic achievements. Always responsible, always trustworthy. I probably couldn't even hit the rim at this point.

The dope had taken all my strength. I mostly just sat on the picnic tables and smoked one USA Gold after another, reading all the names of those who came before me. Mark and Jessica with a heart 2004, Brad and David Ray. Who were these people? Did they find themselves in fourteen days, figure out the error in their ways, and decide to hang it all up for a new way of life? Were Mark and Jessica in love here? Most discussions around the picnic table were about the good old days. Do you know so and so? Did you ever buy off of Roy up Route Seven? I was doing five of them damn things a day!

I was the only one in the treatment facility of my own free will. Most others had come from jail or straight out of the drug court program after a failed urine test. As I looked around at my peers with their rail-thin and broken hands with abscessed knots from missing veins, I saw people desperate for love, even if it was with somebody also in rehab. What happens on day fourteen, when addicts jonesing for drugs are released into the free world? At least the trend was to give people who were addicted the opportunity for help instead of overcrowding the jails with this ever-growing population.

As we sat smoking, wasting the day away, Nathan piped up. "I got some friends coming through on their way to a concert Sunday night. I'm thinking about hopping the fence and going with them."

"Man, you're crazy, you know good and well you will be right back in jail if you do that dumb shit," I said.

"Don't matter. Might as well go enjoy myself. It's always either here or jail. I'm sure they'd take y'all if anybody wants to go."

"I don't know," I said.

"You're stupid if you don't go. You're not even here court ordered. You can walk out right now and not go to jail," he snapped back as he dug his toe into the dirt, unable to make eye contact.

He was right. I couldn't imagine feeling like I was done using, yet I had wasted all my time up until now. I was twenty-five years old and had accomplished nothing in my adult life. All I had learned was how to catch a buzz every day with no source of income. An essential skill in the drug game but not of much use in the real world. Something about being here made me feel secure and safe. As long as I was confined within these walls, I was not getting high, and all the damage I was doing to my family and myself had stopped. The daily grind of stealing and lying and failing in my efforts to live a productive life were on pause. The only problem was that after fourteen days, I had to go back out into the cruel unknown of the real world, and I wasn't sure I was ready for it or the people in it. I wondered if they would let me stay and help others.

Nathan hopped the fence come Sunday night. I never heard from him again.

They told us only 10 percent make it. It was likely that all but one of us would go back out and use. I thought I was the one who would persevere. I'd had the opportunity to leave and get high without immediate repercussions, and I didn't do it. I had stayed. This was my first glimmer of hope.

We walked laps around the inside of the building every morning. Exercise was supposed to be the answer to whatever ailed us. "Mr. Brightside" was on repeat that spring. Music television played videos back then, and that's what we had on most of the time. To this day, when I hear that song, I am transported to that time and place in my life. Although brief, it had a huge impact. It was the first time in a long time I heard people talk about living after years of drug use. It was the first time in a long time I had gone so long without using anything. Never before had I seen or been a part of grown folks removed from society so they could figure out why they couldn't stop compulsively doing something that made them feel so damn good.

Just the sound of that is ludicrous. Sometimes if we were well-behaved, we got off the property for a twelve-step meeting. The only twelve-step meeting in this town was held at the treatment facility once a week, so we often had to go to Whitesburg to attend an outside meeting. Getting acquainted with other people in recovery was that important. On one trip, we stopped at the Isom BP. It was tough being so close to where I grew up. Imagine double doors flying open and out steps a white Econoline van full of patients, squinting and pale like vampires who have just risen and haven't used or been among people for days. I'd scan the parking lot for cars I recognized. I feared conversations that might result from running into someone I knew. Eric's face would have been a welcome sight. It had been weeks since we talked last. Anybody else, and I'd be ducking behind the pop aisle.

Lord, that must have been a sight to behold, and I was right among them. My first dose of humility. Welcome to your feelings. Once, they took us to Natural Bridge State Park to ride the skylift and hike. All these years later, that's my son's favorite place to go. He loves that skylift and those trails. That's because I used those trails as a new way to cope when I got out. I think about my time at Next Step whenever I take him there. But at that moment, we must have looked like something from the movie *Girl, Interrupted*. Here we were, habitual chain-smokers, newly in recovery, out for a day trip. Some people wanted sex, others wanted sweets, but it was safe to say that at this juncture, nobody was intrigued by the idea of replacing their addiction with physical activity.

At the end of my stay, I felt a small glimmer of hope growing in my gut. Would it be possible to navigate the perils of life and not get high no matter what?

The afternoon I was released, I found a meeting and hooked up with some people in recovery. I drive by that building a couple of times a week, and I can see inside at night through the large plate-glass windows. The floor-model TV and couches are gone; they have since been replaced with tables and a podium. I think about the girl who stayed there for two weeks, scared but willing to give life a second chance. I try not to lose sight of where I've been. Now I know it doesn't take a celebrity-named building and twenty-eight days to kick a habit; sleep is not for the weary, and everybody's rock bottom is different.

Birthmark

2010

As I studied my dad's skin, mustard yellow, calloused, and rough, I thought about the matching birthmarks on our legs. On our right legs, mid-thigh, we both had a perfectly round, dime-sized, light-brown pigmentation. A mark he was proud of, one that he pointed out and we studied from as early as I can remember. That wasn't the only mark he left on me. I didn't know then that I would search for the beautiful brown dot on my son's legs as soon as I could get a look at him after he was born. I also didn't know my dad would never leave that hospital bed—his days of freedom and living in the moment ended here.

He was never meant to be old. His spirit was young and magnetic, much too big for an aging body to carry. When I began my recovery in April 2005, they told me I had to change my people, places, and things. My dad was one of those people, and so was Eric. For a year, I stayed away. I was fighting for my life. It was a fight my dad couldn't understand because he had always lived in a manner that catered to his demons. He never knew how to make the hard choices that kept those demons at bay. It wasn't until Amber tracked me down and said, "Your dad is sick, and he wants to see you," that I had to decide.

I had four years with him after he got sick, and I found a way to be with him and stay away from drugs. Now, here we were in this hospital room. He was retaining fluid, and his skin was jaundiced. This is what years of alcohol use looks like. When someone has cirrhosis, their body loses the ability to filter out toxins, and they build up and disrupt all normal functions. The elevated ammonia levels caused him to become disoriented and confused. This time, a stroke had left him in a vegetative state. For four years, I watched him try to quit drinking and smoking, both of which were requirements to get a new liver. He could never sustain either. How could forty-four years of coping be turned around overnight? It was an identity he couldn't live without, a part of his personality that he worried people wouldn't like him without.

He introduced me to the blues: Muddy Waters, Robert Johnson, Lead Belly. He said I had to know where music started to understand where new music came from. We would listen to Stevie Ray Vaughan, Eric Clapton, and the Rolling Stones, and he'd explain how it's all been done before—a masterclass in hearing the hurt. Music was our means of communication. It was something we could discuss at great length. Otherwise, he always felt distant. But when we talked about music, I felt a deep connection.

Because he had no living will or spouse, it was up to me and Chris, my half brother, to decide what to do after the doctors had done all they could. They took us into this room that felt like the air had been sucked out and asked us to put someone else's life in our hands. We pulled the plug with no hope of him waking up or being himself again, pulling the plug on what was keeping him alive, pulling the plug on new memories or songs.

Then there was the wait. Waiting for the last breath, waiting for what I learned was known as the death rattle. When someone gets weaker and begins to lose consciousness, they also lose the ability to clear their throat and swallow. The wet, rattling sound that happens with each breath lets you know the end is near. I couldn't bear to listen. I couldn't stay in that room and hear the life leaving his body. I didn't stay and hold his hand or tell him I loved him. I didn't say goodbye or tell him I forgive him for a childhood that wasn't ordinary. And maybe I should have. Perhaps he would have heard me. But that wasn't our way. But Amber did, until just after midnight on April 1. April

Fool's Day was a day that marked the anniversary of two of his divorces. That man sure could tell a joke.

I was asleep on the love seat in a waiting room just down the hall. I remember the lights were low, which seemed odd for a hospital waiting room. Our family were the only ones there. I don't remember any other patients on that floor. I think they brought us here because they knew he would die. We waited for what seemed like hours. Sitting, standing, taking trips outside to smoke. We told stories because that's what we do. That's where we find comfort. It's funny how the end of someone's life comes down to moments like this. Then, finally, Amber tapped me lightly and said he was gone. At that moment, there was a sense of relief, a feeling that made me feel guilty. As cliché as it sounds, his fight was over. I was sad for our family and for Chris, who had only begun to form a relationship with him. The sadness didn't come to me until much later when I married, graduated college, and had my son. He wasn't here for the second act, the part of my life that came after years of substance use.

We'd only exchanged ill words once that I can remember. He was frustrated at the height of my drug use, and my situation seemed hopeless. I'd called and asked for money, and he didn't have it to give. I was angry, and he fired back with "I never wanted a pill monkey for a daughter." I don't know where he got the term *pill monkey*, but I had only heard him use it in reference to others I knew who struggled with addiction. The disgust that came with those words had never been directed at me. And I responded with "I never wanted a drunk for a daddy." This was one of our last conversations before I went to treatment.

Fortunately, that's not how things ended for us. I had five years clean when he died. I was grateful to be in a better place; I think he knew that. I always knew I wouldn't have him for long, but that doesn't make his leaving any easier. For the average person, fifty-six is middle-aged, a point in your life when you make plans for retirement and life after the daily grind. But it's almost like my dad lived his life in reverse. He never got caught up in a schedule that restricted his freedom. He lived more in those fifty-six years than most people hope to have in eighty. I never saw him worry about a schedule or fret over work deadlines. If it was a Monday and he wanted to ride around and drink, maybe find a place to shoot a game of pool and grab a bite to eat, that's what we did.

There was a sparkle in his eye that dulled after he got sick. I could tell he was living a life he didn't want to live, just as I was finding a new way to live.

Riding in Cars

2010

It was always easier to talk in the car. There was no pressure to make eye contact or read body language. I could grip the steering wheel, and Eric could crack the window to let the cigarette smoke out. We both needed something to do with our hands. The radio could hum quietly in the background. Something about the music in the background made us feel at ease. The same road we traveled all our lives unfolded and required minimal effort. But we weren't doing dope or hunting dope. We were moving our aunt Vicki from Whitesburg to Hindman after the death of her husband. Eric was there to help. He was always there to help. Whether she needed her grass mowed or her dog buried, he was a phone call away. Since my dad's latest stroke, he was the only man around.

I had a few years in recovery, and Eric found himself in drug court after a possession charge. Drug court required weekly drug tests and Narcotics Anonymous meetings. He confessed to me that he was still drinking. At the time, Narcotics Anonymous was a critical part of my recovery. I could tell that maybe he hadn't bought into the culture of recovery. But NA, like anything else, is about the people it's made up of and designed so that one particular group or area doesn't define the organization. I could tell he hadn't found his people. After attending a meeting the day I left treatment, it was suggested to attend at least one meeting every day for the first year. That's how old-timers in NA tell you what worked for them. They give it to you in suggestions. Addicts can be stubborn and think they know what works best for them. So telling them what to do can often lead to them doing the opposite. I attended a meeting every day for the first year. I never missed a day. Some days I'd hit two.

It was also suggested that I find a higher power. I didn't grow up with any religious background. But it seemed to me this was a good thing. It allowed me to recover in a space where I knew my actions were the result of a disease and not some moral failure on my part. I saw many people with substance use disorder dealing with the baggage of a god-fearing upbringing. I began a deep dive into all the organized religions, searching for a higher power that I could relate to, something greater than myself I could believe in and trust. I read everything I could get my hands on.

I checked out book after book from the library and spent endless hours researching what I thought was the perfect fit for me. I read books on Buddhism and Scientology, practiced the art of Zen meditation. I tagged along with some of my closest friends in recovery who participated in Native American ceremonies. Nothing really stuck. But experience in recovery has taught me that if I do the right thing for the right reason, unexplainable things happen for me. And that's all the higher power I needed. That was the same year I cut off all contact with my dad's side of the family, including Eric. I was about to celebrate five years clean. Narcotics Anonymous introduced me to a new way of life and a new way of thinking. The members of NA were my friends, and NA functions were my social life. I had to change a lot in the beginning. I didn't go to concerts much early on, as much as I loved them. I was afraid of getting high. NA and my life after felt regimented and routine. After a life in active addiction, I longed for something to happen, anything to happen. Something that would evoke those old feelings, but it was hard to get to that place again. It was like my brain couldn't muster up that amount of joy on its own.

I stayed away from all the places and people I associated with getting high. Social anxiety was also a real struggle. Crippling anxiety attacks plagued me, and I never knew when they were coming. I hadn't learned to function in the world without being high, but I kept trying with the hope that it would get better one day. The alternative was to continue masking the pain, which I knew didn't work. This was the crossroads at which Eric and I both found ourselves.

For the first time, driving around that day, we talked about the blushing. I was aware of it, and he was aware of it. I knew it rarely happened when we talked to each other, but I saw it happening whenever we spoke to anyone else. I remember him saying on this car ride, "I don't know how to do it without a beer or something." I knew the *it* he was referring to was anything social. All I could offer was my experience. I was still awkward. My face still turned red. I'd found a group of people that made this less of a struggle, a community that accepted me and could see my qualities despite my flaws and less-than-perfect past.

Addicts are passionate, sensitive, creative, and intuitive by nature. These attributes often led us to use in the first place. But if we are fortunate enough to get into recovery and spend time getting to the core of our true selves, these qualities put us in positions we would never dream possible. Addicts in recovery are some of the most genuine people I know. They don't have time for bullshit. It's a matter of life or death. We get fed a lot of storylines about people in active addiction, and it gives us an air of hopelessness. But I know from experience, freedom from addiction is possible, and to hear about the personal and spiritual growth of those in recovery is refreshing. The recovery process is a blessing in disguise because you soon find out drugs were not the problem. As the fog rolls out, you see yourself again for the first time. We feel deeply and respond accordingly; sometimes, that's not pretty. We often operate on stunted emotional maturity, leading to many uncomfortable emotions and nowhere to put them. Coping skills are stripped, and what's left is raw and insecure.

I tried to explain to Eric all the things recovery had given me. I could hold down a job, people could trust me again, and I could go through the day without that gnawing feeling inside. I was recovering by working the twelve steps, allowing myself to be vulnerable, reversing old patterns, and healing trauma. After I'd been in recovery for about a year, I took a job at Walmart, which was hard for me. It required a level of humility that I needed to stay away from drugs. When I saw people I knew while I was working, I hid in the back because I was ashamed. I thought I should be doing more with my life. I thought I was capable of more. These people had seen me high for years, but I no longer had the crutch of drugs. My ego had been stripped. I couldn't find it in me to be proud that I was in recovery. I didn't feel like that was enough. Those lessons were hard and uncomfortable, but I knew if I stayed in recovery, it would get better.

After Walmart, I took a job with an environmental firm out of Louisville that had just opened an office in Hazard. They wanted to get into the coal business and needed someone local, someone familiar with the region, who could help them get a foot in the door. That really meant someone who could speak the language. I felt good about that work. I was sampling old and new retention ponds and potential surface and well-water contamination. All those years of trying to go to college, this was the dream I was chasing—so staying in recovery was opening doors. But in the end, you have to want it and be willing to sit in emotions you've spent years running from. That's a hard thing to do. Me being in recovery would never be enough. I couldn't save us both. I could do all the work, but I was the only one that could reap the rewards.

I wanted to stop that car, grab him by the face, and say, "Dammit, do it. Eric, do the work. You're going to die. You don't have to live like this. Forget taking care of everyone around you, and do something for yourself. Let go of our family's toxic past. Be the one who breaks the cycle." But he wasn't ready to hear that. And the car ride between Whitesburg and Hindman wasn't long enough. We didn't have enough road left to get into that.

Wednesday, January 16, 2013

We were having a soup bean dinner at Aunt Vicki's. I had been looking forward to it because we didn't get together much anymore. Since I got clean and Eric continued to do whatever it was he was doing, we hadn't had a chance to be together like we used to. I missed our carefree days together. I took these family dinners and holiday gatherings and considered them a blessing that we were both around to tell the tale and grateful that we had each other.

It was cold and overcast. On days like those, it feels like I can never get warm. The mountains are unforgiving this time of year; everything is lifeless and gray, and it's hard to remember how green and beautiful spring will be when the trillium and pink lady's slippers ease up from the ground.

At work, it was all I could do to sit in the office all day. When I took that job, I was sampling retention ponds all over eastern Kentucky for an environmental lab out of Louisville. I enjoyed being outside and on the move, but it turned out that I don't do well with sedentary gigs. I felt like I was serving the greater good by keeping an eye on the coal industry and ensuring they adhered to environmental regulations.

Sometimes it felt like life had come full circle and I was back on these strip jobs, just like when Eric and I were kids, just like when I was running from everything in my youth. My relationship with these mountains is intimate. I have seen their every detail. I have seen all the nuanced patterns of their inside—just as they have seen mine.

The day of the soup bean dinner, I got a message from Amber, telling me that Eric hadn't been responding to her text invite to dinner. I went ahead and shot him a text because I knew he'd respond to me. The day went on with no response. Worry began to creep in. Our family feared the worst. Somewhere inside, I started to feel the truth. It started with a lump in my throat and the constant repetition of "Why isn't he answering?" the way a song gets stuck in your head. They all assumed he was on a bender somewhere, holed up and getting high, lost in the euphoria, and unable to return a message. I knew that wasn't true. I couldn't recall one time in our lives when he didn't answer me. As I made my trek to Hindman that evening, the dinner he wouldn't show up for, deep down, I knew he was gone. A cold mist fell from the air, and the trees without leaves were haunting the mountains, uninviting. As we sat around the table, everyone tried to write this off as something it was not. I kept my thoughts to myself. Twelve hours, and no one had heard from him.

Thursday, January 17, 2013

The day began with pictures of Eric and his truck circulating on social media, holding out hope that somebody, somewhere, had seen or heard from him. The fact that he wasn't texting back or responding to the droves of people posting on Facebook was alarming. He didn't show up for work for two days in a row, which affirmed everything I already knew. No way in hell would he miss work and not tell anyone.

At times, his drug use was worse than others, and even in those times, he showed up for his commitments. Messages started rolling in from various sources, some of which I thought I could trust, others that seemed like disillusioned paranoia. We followed up on all of them. Word started circulating that Eric and his live-in girlfriend had a falling out on Tuesday night, and he left. From there, he hooked up with an old acquaintance and possibly a couple of female companions. I showed up for work and trudged on as if my world wasn't on the verge of destruction. By noon, I figured out I was useless there, so Amber, Courtney, and I decided our time would be better served searching.

I'm not sure what we were searching for, Eric's body or our peace of mind, so we spent the day in every holler he'd been known to haunt in the far reaches of Knott County. It was still cold, and it was still raining. Every one-lane paved road turned gravel ended with no more information than when we started. We made a complete loop: Branham's Creek, Pinetop, Beaver, Garner, Jones Fork, and finally, Garrett. By now, we felt confident that the story about the women working at the Garrett Quick Mart was true and that this dude he was with may have killed him.

We had been told he was last seen in Triplett Branch, so at the edge of dark, we headed that way. There was a churning in my gut as we turned off the main highway onto an unfamiliar road in an unfamiliar part of the county. The vibe changed as the road turned from asphalt to gravel, and discomfort filled the car. This must be what outsiders feel when they find themselves in the hollers of central Appalachia after years of hearing tales about toothless banjo players and feuds that break out at a moment's notice. But that isn't my Appalachia at all. I find comfort in the roads leading to a mountain's top. A place I associate with freedom and glorious views. Miles of gently rolling peaks and narrow valleys. A place that makes me proud of where I'm from, a place that makes me wonder how or why a person would want to live anywhere else. But that sense of freedom also gives way to a place to hide, and sometimes no good can come from needing to hide.

There weren't many houses. A few single-wide trailers lined the sides of the road, the windows glowing with light as afternoon turned to night. Families inside went about their business, making dinner and doing homework—families alive and well, with plans for tomorrow. As dark settled, the road became a narrow strip of gravel; the mine access road and darkness had shut out all the light. We started talking about how it was late, and we didn't know exactly what we were looking for or where we were going. But I knew the truth. The truth that there was a good possibility he was here. Or at least, evidence that he was there. And without saying it out loud, we all knew that we didn't want to be the ones to find him. That's the kind of trauma one doesn't recover from, the kind that changes you on a molecular level. DNA shifting and adapting to make room for the pain that used to be joy. At that moment, we decided to turn around and start again fresh the next day. Twenty-four hours, and no one had heard from him.

Friday, January 18, 2013

I was lost in speculation. Homicide detectives were involved. The guys Eric worked with found his truck that morning in Triplett Branch, yards from where we had been the night before. I thought about where I would be if we had found that truck. Eric's truck, a black Dodge Ram, covered in blood splatter from God only knows what kind of brutal scene. Was he scared, in pain, and confused? What were his last thoughts? Did he know this was the end, or was it swift and painless? I guess I was in shock, emotionless, and processing. I had been rehearsing the pain of him leaving for days now.

At three o'clock that afternoon, the Kentucky State Police employed the help of a helicopter to get an aerial view of the scene. Initial attempts to find his body failed. Flipping through old photos at his mom's house, our family tried to find comfort in the good times. We were all gathered there, waiting. Impending doom . . . we all knew it was coming. We didn't know when. The cigarette smoke was thick, and the air smelled stale.

His poor mom hadn't slept well. After hours of waiting, I was going home to get some rest—whatever form rest took now. On the ride home, I left the interior light of my car on. I was scared, and the comfort of a night-light seemed to help. I was thirty-two years old. I made the trek thirty miles back to Hazard only to turn around as soon as I got there. Amber called. They found the body, alone beside the creek. A creek that's shallow, making its way down the mountain and out of the holler. All his belongings were stripped, including his cell phone and wallet. Alone again, night-light, life forever changed. Facing the reality of the situation.

Saturday, January 19, 2013

Where do I go from here?

SONGS I WISH YOU KNEW
2013–2020

Uneasy

2013

Once Eric was gone, I could not do the dishes. At the sink, I felt his presence behind me. My hands submerged in the warm soapy water, the sun streaking through the window warming my face, even in mid-January. But there was a slight shift in pressure, a change in the room's acoustics. My arm hair stood up, and my skin exploded into goose bumps. Someone was behind me, and there was not a doubt in my mind that someone was Eric. I didn't mention this in my weekly therapy sessions.

I wanted to believe that he was trapped between life as we know it on Earth and whatever awaits us on the other side. Maybe he had a piece of unfinished business, like paranormal investigators always talk about. I wanted him here to guide me. I didn't want to let go. I don't particularly believe in an afterlife, so the probability that his spirit might have stuck around seems natural to me.

My days at home were long and uncomfortable. I navigated my house like a battleground, with my back to the wall. I filled my days with mindless errands around town or long lunch dates with friends. I've heard others talk about their paranormal experiences as calming.

I wouldn't describe these encounters as calming. I did whatever it took to keep my mind occupied. I wondered if I had finally lost it this time. When someone asked how I was doing, I gave a fake answer. The statute of limitations for grief seems extremely short. I knew when they asked, they didn't want to know. They would get uncomfortable and shift around, put their hands in their pockets, and stare at the ground while I told them that everyone was getting along just fine. Somehow, all this was more palatable to everyone because we had a body to bury and someone to put behind bars.

There was no trial. Jerry confessed and took a plea deal that dropped the charge from murder to manslaughter. Jerry was an old acquaintance, someone Eric trusted. Some might even use the word friend.

I went into the courtroom that day ready to hear the truth, ready to see Eric's murderer on trial and brought to justice. But there would be no trial—only a sentencing. My aunt Jenny had the opportunity to address Jerry that day. She told the story of how Eric liked to fix broken toys when he was little. How he kept that philosophy throughout his life, how he wanted to fix what was broken. Eric was a helper until the end.

Amber and I obtained the discovery packet from his case, which included testimony given by the two girls Eric and Jerry were with that night and the medical examiner's report. The girls said Jerry was making unwanted advances and Eric was trying to protect them, making an already intoxicated Jerry angry. And he took it out on Eric. The girls fled on foot, and he was left there to defend himself, unarmed, against an attacker with a knife. Left for dead after multiple stab wounds.

Medical Examiner Receipt for Personal Effects/Evidence

- DNA Card
- Boxer Shorts
- Jeans
- Boots, Red Wing (no socks present)
- Nine (9) cigarette butts from left front pocket

Fifteen years in exchange for a life. That sure doesn't feel like justice. They will never understand the truth about what murder does to the living.

I would wake up, soaked in sweat, my heart racing, afraid of the dark, and flooded with emotion. I've never been to war, but I imagine this inconsolable state I found myself in night after night must be something akin to PTSD that veterans feel. I would wake up my husband and dump all these graphic images on him because I couldn't carry this burden alone. He listened, and I cried. He held me, and we turned on the television as a distraction. I moved through my days from one distraction to the next. Is this what being in mourning is—a long line of diversions? It was hard to differentiate dreams from reality. The emotional gut punch felt real to me. When I fell asleep at night, I watched as my subconscious unfolded.

It's me in the police station in what looks like the interrogation room from every cop show I've seen. The detectives stand around, sipping coffee from paper cups and carefully taking notes. I'm seated at a table with a single light bulb swinging overhead, shadowing all the faces around me. Eric's mom is inconsolable and angry. She wants answers. Their plan to find out what happened is to put me in his mind, à la John Malkovich. I'm upset and resistant to this whole idea. I beg, plead, and tell them they can't do this to me. The cops try to convince me that this is the only way we will ever discover what happened. That Eric would want it this way.

This is what I wake to regularly now. I must convince myself that it was only a dream. The emotions are so natural and intense that it is hard to separate them from reality. They are reality.

My grief has finally had time to breathe. I don't feel Eric around anymore. But sometimes, like at Christmas and the anniversary of his death, when I'm in the car alone in the dark and the music is up, I get a shiver in my spine and that same shift in vibration that leads me to believe someone is occupying my back seat. So, I flip on the overhead light and ride that way for a long while, until I'm comfortable again. I never talk out loud to whoever is around; I sometimes talk in my mind, whole conversations. I eventually came clean to my therapist and told a few family members I was convinced he was haunting me. And when this book sees the light of day, the world will know.

If Eric did stick around, if he was trying to tell me something, I hope it was to let me know he was okay. That what happened to him wasn't so bad. That I can make it without him. This whole experience makes me wonder if this was all in my head or if there is a period after we die when we are in limbo until the energy from our bodies can finally rest. I wonder how tragedy and the way you die affects how you leave.

I've gone back to the place where Eric was murdered. Turning off the main road onto a single-lane paved road and, eventually, a dirt road that climbs to the top of the mountain. The place feels unsettled. The single-wide trailers that frame both sides make me uneasy, like someone is peering out the windows but can't be seen. The holler gives off an aura of being watched, even when no one is around. I've walked the ground where his truck was parked. I've seen the evidence bags and gloves left over by the cops. I know the exact location where his body was found. I know how his hands were partially submerged in water in the creek that meanders its way between the mountains. I can't help but think how it was January and bitterly cold, how the rain came down nonstop that week. I wonder how long he had to lay there before he was finally gone. I wonder if he was running away from his attacker or unconscious and slipped down the hill. These are the things I would ask if that ghost in my back seat could talk.

Running Down a Dream

2020

From my window at the bookshop on the corner, I saw people like him every day. I wondered if he had a home. I wondered if he had anybody who cared where he'd sleep tonight. That's something that's changed since Eric's been gone. The people who are homeless. We are at least two, in some cases three, generations deep in the opioid epidemic. People lost their family homes, and there was no one to fall back on when times got hard. People lived on the streets, and the faces changed every day.

We made eye contact, and he reached for the door handle. He stopped outside, just short of the door, and finished his cigarette, folding a bandanna into a makeshift mask. His clothes were clean, and he was wearing a backpack. I was cautious, and that made me feel judgmental. Right away, he commented that I sell Ale-8-One: "I like this place already," pointing to the mini fridge. He said he remembered when my store was on Main Street, but he never stopped in.

The silence sat awkwardly between us. He was struggling to make eye contact, and I noticed his hands were red and swollen. It was unseasonably warm, so he was wearing a T-shirt. I saw knots under the skin in the bends of his arm. We struck up a conversation about a Tom Petty book. He threw out the term *memoir*, which caught me off guard. He told me about the daughter of a woman he was staying with, how she was an artist. Would I consider hanging her work in the store? He knew she was good because his girlfriend had her paintings hanging around the house.

I wondered what her house looked like. I pictured it with a mattress on the floor, clothes thrown about, scarcely furnished. And then there were the paintings and canvases, too small and oddly proportioned compared to the wall. I agreed to give her a shot and some space in the store to sell her work. Maybe that's what she needed. I went back to his use of a literary term for which I didn't give him credit. He told me he wished someone had helped him. He wished for a do-over. I could see myself where he stood that day. I had that chance. I had that do-over.

I think about Eric and his situation and how a do-over would have been impossible for him with everyone around him still struggling with addiction. There are a lot of tough decisions in those early years of recovery. Staying away from people you know and love, opening yourself up to strangers, and learning to trust. Trusting when you haven't been able to trust anyone in years. Maybe you've never trusted anyone at all.

I was lucky to have my mom. She wasn't my biggest fan then, but she gave me a place to land and one year without working so I could focus solely on my recovery. That year was the most valuable year of my life. It opened the door to everything happening now, including this book in your hands and my bookstore on the corner. Early on, I stayed clean to please everyone around me. Many people invested time and resources in my recovery, and I didn't want to disappoint them. I was so tired of letting people down. The people-pleasing kicked in because it's all I'd ever known. I had to be good and do good so they would love me. At some point, though, I started staying clean for me. I wouldn't sabotage myself for fear of failure. I'd trust the process and relinquish control. The days got easier.

I should have been nervous, maybe apprehensive, that he was there. He picked up a Stephen King book and told me his favorite serial is the *Green Mile* series. I could tell he was a reader. Probably like a lot of others who suffer with addiction, the type of personality that becomes obsessed with hobbies and new topics. The kind that becomes so passionate that they must learn it all. So talented and so sensitive.

I was curious about how often he wanted to look around inside. I wondered if he was only there now to escape the rain.

"How much for this one?" he asked as he held the Tom Petty book in his hands, carefully rubbing the cover, black and white, with a photograph of Tom taking up the front. Then, he began flipping through the pages.

"Twenty-eight ninety-five," I said as I went to show him some cheaper paperbacks I had in stock. It was presumptuous of me to think he didn't have the money for that book. Instead, he decided on an Ale-8 and an *Odyssey* button for his backpack. His wallet was worn black leather and was connected to his belt by a chain. It reminded me of the black leather jacket my dad sent me from Florida, which I gave to Eric. He dug around until he found a folded twenty deep in a side pocket. I wondered how long that twenty had to last him. As I rang him up and began to make the change, he told me about joining LinkedIn because the job market around here was so tough.

"Already found me one that pays people to write reviews about hunting equipment." He looked up and made eye contact when he began to talk about writing. "It's only four hundred words weekly, and you can work from home. Sounds like a dream gig to me." I heard the tone of his voice shift.

I handed over his change. He didn't seem to notice that I didn't charge him any sales tax. I'd eat the twenty cents.

"Did you know Coca-Cola sued Ale-8 for making a pop similar to theirs?"

I need to find out if this tidbit of information is accurate, but he didn't seem to be the bullshitting type so far.

"I never knew they made anything like a cola," I said as I watched him fasten the button to his pack.

I hate that he was forty-four, and this could be it for him. Bouncing around from couch to couch, putting needles in his arm, and having to love everything from afar. I wished I could buy that Tom Petty book for him. I wished I could give it to him with no repercussions. As he turned to go, he said he'd be back to support small businesses. He liked having something like this downtown. I wished there were a way I could do something to help him. But out the door and up the street, it was pouring rain, something I seemed more concerned about than him. I'd like to know if he'd read *The Odyssey*.

Grey Goose Chandelier

2020

I went to a bar to pick up dinner. The cash register was in the back. I was now officially in the bowels of someone's Saturday night. It used to be my Saturday night. TVs of all shapes and sizes playing the Kentucky game, and Johnny Lang's "Lie to Me" was just loud enough. There was something about the pain in his voice that cut deeper than it did when I was seventeen. Did I know anything about the blues back then? The crowd was mostly men, but it was not uncomfortably full, especially given that we were deep in a pandemic.

A woman sat at the end of the bar where I was paying. She was slightly overweight and appeared to be alone. The men sitting closest to her were having a conversation about losing the sense of taste and smell and how that affected their affinity for food and drink. The bartender laughed and asked, "Can I get you another one?" The man nodded his head as if they had developed their own language. The woman's demeanor didn't change. I could smell the Michelob Light she was sipping. I had a gut reaction to a smell I knew so well. One that only came my way on occasion now but remained ingrained for a lifetime. Waiting for my order, I tried to focus on anything but the voice in my head telling me it was okay for me to drink now. I was almost forty. It's been sixteen years, and I'm different, more responsible. I could control this if I wanted to.

These are thoughts I never had early in recovery. I was determined to stay clean. Early on, I remembered the pain, I battled the guilt and shame associated with my drug use. I could see light coming in, but I knew what the prison of addiction felt like. I started my day with the NA meditation. I set my intention and focus for the day based on that reading. I texted others in recovery or called my sponsor to secure meeting plans for that evening. I was a diligent step worker. My feelings and shortcomings would pour out onto the page. I desperately wanted to rid myself of the past and the desire to use drugs. It felt a lot like when I started writing about Eric. The relief I found in writing early on in Narcotics Anonymous became my only outlet time and time again. NA consumed my life.

When I wasn't at work, I was in a meeting or with others in recovery. When I had the appropriate amount of clean time, I got involved in the regional service structure of NA. People trusted me again, and that gave me confidence. I never thought about getting high. I remember the night when I realized something inside me had changed. I was working third shift at Walmart. I had a little over a year clean, and another employee approached me with a bottle of pills—one of those times when an addict knows another instinctively. I had no prior relationship with this person. He asked if I wanted a couple of Percocets. That night was the first time I had been offered drugs since getting clean.

On the outside, I was calm. On the inside, anxiety was taking over. I blew the guy off and ran to the bathroom, heart racing, sweating. My lips were numb, and my ears felt like they were stuffed with cotton. I was scared. Never in my life had I been scared of a bottle of pills. For years, that's where I found my only relief. But I was different then. After I regained my composure, I felt stronger. A fellow person in recovery was also working there. I explained to her what had happened, putting those new coping skills to work. I could have sat on that information alone all night, maybe talked myself into thinking it was okay to do just one. But instead, I reached out, a skill foreign to me, something I must work hard to do even now. The voice in my head still says I'm being dramatic or that no one cares or that

I'm being a burden. But I got through that night, and I didn't get high, and I didn't get high the night I was offered a joint at a Rolling Stones concert, and I didn't get high the night someone offered me a drink at a Jason Isbell show. And I didn't get high when my grandpa died, or when my dad died, or when Eric died. I built a strong foundation in NA, took all the suggestions, and did the work obsessively. I showed up and did it one day at a time, and my life was different. When I think about it now, it seems uneventful: work, meetings, and coffee. But I was out of the chaos and into a safe space.

But the lack of chaos gave room for feelings to creep in. There were still a lot of intense emotions, and I felt hopeless at times that I had nowhere to put them. But as the NA saying goes, "Feelings are not fact," so I'd have to sit with them uncomfortably until they subsided. I replaced drugs with what I see now were healthy distractions. We had functions for all the major holidays and a campout in the summer. The members of Narcotics Anonymous became my family. It was a relief to find myself surrounded by people who knew what it was like and how it felt to be addicted. They understand that part of an addict always feels alone and not quite like everybody else. People who weren't afraid to get really honest and face things head-on, knowing if they searched for an escape, it would cause nothing but pain.

I looked at the chandelier, crafted from old Grey Goose bottles. I looked at the bottles of liquor that lined the shelves. The lady with the Michelob left the comfort of her barstool to go to the restroom.

I watched a bead of sweat slowly glide down the front of her bottle. I could see its path as it reached the bottom. Singing behind my mask, the memories associated with this song flashed through my mind like slides from a lousy vacation. Memories of holding a bottle and not holding back. Drinking way before I was twenty-one, crowded around the kitchen table at a house party. Filling some hole inside of me that I couldn't bear witness to at such a young age. Doing it out of necessity, not because I thought I looked cool. Doing it because it was what my family did. I made trips to barrooms just like this as a kid with my dad. He would instantly take over a room. By the time we left, he had made friends with everybody he came in contact with.

"Ma'am, your card." A voice jolted me back. Back to the present and out of the past. I grabbed my order, and left, but not without an alteration to my core. Was it the pandemic that had me longing for a connection? Had this longing for a connection always been there? Was that need for a connection the ultimate reason why? In the car on the way home, home to the life I'd made, safe and secure without the trials and tribulations of addiction, Johnny Lang sings "Lie to Me."

Epilogue

2024

I've been in recovery longer than I got high. How I got here has been a strange, almost serendipitous journey. One that's hard to explain. It's like when I decided to get clean, everything fell into place. I'm not saying the past eighteen years have been easy, but I always have this feeling that things will work out. After Eric was murdered, I took some time off from the world. I stayed home for seven years. I took care of my son, Tripp, and finished college. More important, I grieved. I gave myself the time and space to process a loss I thought would consume me forever. I remedied my pain with food and naps. I got lost in schoolwork, hiking, and being a mom.

And most important, writing. Writing became the ultimate release. I walked straight through the pain. I didn't drink, smoke pot, or reach for pills. Grief is isolating and painful. But writing became the place I found comfort. I found myself coming back to the things I loved, like reading and live music. There's so much music I wish Eric was around to hear. I just attended my tenth Jason Isbell show. His music is like taking a page out of my journal. Eric would have loved his live shows, and I think about him whenever I go—when he hits a solo reminiscent of the Allman Brothers or Neil Young. I want to turn to Eric for confirmation that he heard it too. The funny part is his songs I love the most are about addiction and loss. It's as if his music came along right when I needed it, and I wonder, if Eric were still around, if it would feel the same way for him.

Now, I spend most of my days in the bookstore I own in Hazard, Kentucky. I look at my life and wonder how I wound up here. It feels strange and exactly right all at the same time. So many times, I wanted to give up on life, through grief, social anxieties, and addiction. The weight of living seemed too much to bear, but the cost of leaving was always too high. After I opened the bookstore, my network continued to grow, putting me in situations where I'm forced to pause and reflect, situations I often don't feel worthy of. That make me feel like an imposter. Someone like me wasn't supposed to become a leader in the community. Someone shy and introspective who feared saying the wrong thing and speaking her mind. Maybe it's how I was raised. My thoughts and ideas never had room to grow. So, these feelings keep coming up on this road of figuring out where I belong. My journey has been one of mistakes, one of guilt and shame, and one of triumphs.

Even after all this time in recovery, I still have moments that remind me of the crazy shit I did. A friend of mine asked me to be the bookseller at his book launch. Due to the ongoing supply chain issues in the publishing industry because of Covid, I found out days before the event that my order of 150 books would not be filled in time to make the event. Through some last-minute maneuvers, I secured the order directly from the publisher. After a long weekend of watching and tracking the packages across the US, I had to arrange a meeting beside the road with my UPS driver. At the final hour, I received the order and made the event. Relief.

This got me thinking about when I ordered pills online. A time that doesn't feel so long ago when, in reality, it's been twenty years. Chasing down a UPS driver to secure a package of pills being mailed from Miami before they made it to my home address so my mom wouldn't know. It's unbelievable how an online survey could land me 90 Lortabs and 120 Xanax. It must have been hell for the UPS drivers having a bunch of addicts flagging them down all over town. In an area already oversaturated with pills from an industry that made pain its priority, so much so that it was deemed the fifth vital sign, we took it upon ourselves to get more shipped in. There was never enough. But a sense of security and relief followed meeting the UPS driver. For a fleeting moment, it felt like everything would be okay. If there was a stream of pills, the dread, anxiety, and impending sickness all felt miles away.

Not so far off from the feeling of getting my books on time. I can follow through on a promise after days of agonizing over letting someone I respect and admire down. After years of not showing up, not for myself or anyone around me, it's times like these that can send me into a tailspin. I try hard to avoid situations that make me feel like a disappointment. These are the memories that remain no matter how many years clean or how many moments I've made the right choice.

That baggage from the past lingers in the background, a reminder of where I came from and how close I always am to being there again.

The Last of the Two of Us

Eric,

Tripp was six months old when you died. Immediately, I was grateful for the one picture I had of you two together. Sitting on the couch at Vicki's, Tripp gripping your thumb. You are both blond-haired and blue-eyed, looking up at the camera. I'll never forget you saying, "He is a little brute. Gonna make Mandi millions as a linebacker."

That gratitude was balanced with regret. Regret that you would never know each other. Regretting the time I missed with you after I got clean and everything changed. You knew I had to keep a safe distance. I had to avoid the people and places I associated with getting high.

We both know our relationship was so much more than that.

Keeping that distance suited me well. Until you died. I felt guilty for not being there when you needed me. The night you died, I wondered if you would have called me instead of Jerry if we had been as close as we were in the past. Could you have vented your frustrations to me? Would I have been a haven? I always felt better knowing you were in the world somewhere, even if we didn't talk every day, just knowing there was someone I could depend on. Someone who loved me unconditionally. That gave me comfort.

Even if you were using, I knew I could count on you for anything. I'm not sure you felt the same way about me by that point.

I got the impression that you felt abandoned when I got clean. That I couldn't understand what you were going through anymore. But you respected my journey and guarded me against anything you were using. And this created a space between us. I know it's hard for people in active addiction to maintain their relationships with people who aren't getting high anymore. I somehow thought we were different, but ultimately it kept us apart.

I also consider the other side. What if I hadn't gotten clean? Would I have been there that night? Would I have witnessed your death or even been killed? I wasn't with you during any of your near-death experiences, and every time I wondered how things would have been different if I had been there. Sometimes I think about the eight years between when I got clean and your death. I long for the time that seems wasted. Time that we didn't get to spend together. If I could go back and change anything, it would be that. I would have tried to see you instead of being consumed with recovery.

But I was scared, and I desperately wanted this to work. It was life or death, Eric. And decisions like that come with hefty price tags. As we got older, I knew things would change. Adult obligations cut into youthful freedoms. And I thought the more clean time I got, the easier it would be for us to hang out again. I'd get better at identifying triggers and my emotional state. I thought there would be more time. No one else was looking out for you.

We were told early on to look out for each other. But was it realistic to think that would keep us safe forever?

I wondered if you had someone to talk to. Someone you could trust. I had to make all new friends. Friends who made their recovery a top priority. I had to get used to sharing my feelings in public. Every night around a table full of people in recovery. Lots of coffee and cigarettes. I never wanted to preach to you, but I thought the changes in my life would help you make the necessary changes in yours. But getting clean is hard, and staying clean is even harder.

After you died, I missed being together and reminiscing. You starting every story with "Remember that time . . ." I became the keeper of all those stories. Everybody was gone—you, Daddy, David, my papaw. Part of me was convinced I would forget everything. That my life before your death would suddenly disappear.

When I'd put Tripp to bed at night, I'd sit in his nursery in the dark. The white-noise machine in the shape of a giraffe filled the silence. My laptop became conversations with you. I started telling myself those stories, capturing them so they would never disappear. And they poured out effortlessly. I'd type long after Tripp was asleep. I did this for months after you were gone—years after you were gone. Anytime something triggered a memory. Anytime I needed to feel close to you. In that space, I felt peace and unconditional love. The type of love I didn't know was possible again until I became a mother. There was something about sitting in front of a glowing laptop after a long day that put me at ease, that made me feel like I was sharing my day with you. Tripp's soul felt like ours, and as he grunted and rocked himself to sleep, I knew that part of what I was writing was for him. I didn't think I could ever tell him in a way that he would fully understand who you were. But I could write about our life together, and maybe then he could see. He would come to realize the bond and how we needed each other.

After you died, something inside me died too. A light that died for a long time. I began to see the world differently. Suddenly, I understood the importance of people. Maybe this is what grief does. It forces us to see what's meaningful in our lives. Without you, I didn't want to run a race of constant work and the acquisition of things. I wanted close, intimate conversations in spaces that make me happy, like how we grew up. I had nothing to lose after I lost you. Your death broke me. But I couldn't sit and be a broken person. I had been that person, and I wanted more. Tripp deserved more. You and I know better than anyone what it's like being raised by broken people.

Those stories I wrote in the dark after you died opened doors for me that I didn't even know existed. It was the only way I knew to cope. I started sharing those stories with other people. And somewhere along the way, I started writing about myself and what it was like getting high for all those years. People wanted to hear them for whatever reason, so I kept writing them. And now I'm surrounded by writers. Oddly enough, I found them in eastern Kentucky at the Hindman Settlement School. It's wild going back there now. I think about all the times we drove past there and had no idea what was happening. We knew nothing about the writers that convene there every summer. Being at Hindman with those writers was the first time I felt at home since you've been gone. It felt like the parties at David's, where everybody sat around and told stories, and then somebody would get out a guitar and start picking, and everybody sang. It felt like family. You could just be who you were. So, after my first year at the writers' workshop, I decided to open a bookstore in Hazard. I loved these people and their writing so much, and it made such an impact on me I wanted to share it with the world. Never in a million years could I have imagined all this. You wouldn't believe it, Eric.

But in some ways, the life I've created since your death feels like a trade-off. Like I had to lose you to find me. To find my voice. In your absence, I began to understand the importance of our story, not only to me but to others.

I miss you every day. Especially the first days of spring, when the sun is warm but there's a chill in the air. There is something about the sun on days like these. How it warms up the car. And that contrast makes me forget how dark the winters are.

Today I left work early. It was the first warm day we've had since fall. I got that itchy feeling, as you do when the seasons change. I wanted nothing more than to pick you up and ride with the windows down. We could play some Rolling Stones and smoke cigarettes. And you could talk about Charlie Watts's sheepish grin and effortless drumming. We could sing "Miss You" in horrible British accents. So, I did it anyway. The sun made me feel alive again, so I left work, got in the car, and rolled down the windows. And I sang loud, and I smiled, and I cried at the same time. Because I can. Because I'm still here.

Now when our family gets together, I can see the look on our cousin Amber's face. Part nostalgia, part pain. The look that says, "Eric should be here." There should be a little version of you that runs around playing with the little versions of us. Stair-step cousins like we were. Amber and I are moms now, which is weird but feels right at the same time. I think about you whenever we take our boys up on a strip job. All the strip mines around here have wild horses on them now, so we take them to feed the horses and have a picnic. No booze or cigarettes, but I still keep the music cranked up. And it feels the same. We roll the windows down, and the dust gets in. Miles of flat land where flat land was never meant to be. With the coal industry all but gone, these boys don't even know how the landscape got this way. But they don't care. They are just happy to be together. When I watch them share a language of their own and make up games to play, I remember you. I'm happy for them, but I remember you. And I know how important these relationships are. They may not realize it now, but someday, they will.

Tripp was so little when you died, and I was so full of grief. I worried that my emotional state would have lasting effects on him. I think I did okay. I think I'm an okay mom. I try to introduce him to great music, but he resists. I guess that makes me an old person. He'll say, "No offense, Mommy, but your music sucks." And I feel the same about his. I love him like crazy. He's funny, creative, and has a heart of gold. That big heart worries me sometimes because I've seen that before. You know what it's like to care too much. He's constantly aware of everyone around him and how they feel. He always wants to be good and never wants to disappoint anyone. What he doesn't know is he probably saved me. I would have gotten high when you died if it hadn't been for him. I missed you in a way that I didn't know existed. Pain that I had nowhere to go with. With eight years clean, I had a lot to lose if I sought out a temporary escape.

I've been in recovery for eighteen years now, and still, the stakes are even higher. The drugs are different now. They don't even make OxyContin anymore. It took years, but people finally caught on to the damage all those pain pill prescriptions caused. But that left a whole bunch of people addicted with no dope to do. So now it's street drugs, a lot of heroin and meth, and it's potent and killing people. The thought of a relapse at this point is scary. It always was, but the possibility of an overdose is real. So real that they've developed an antidote. Narcan. One shot of this nasal spray, and it brings people back. Addicts are carrying it around. It's part of using these days. They have to because just about all the dope is cut with fentanyl, a synthetic opioid much more potent than anything we ever did.

It's hard to believe that it got worse after OxyContin. At the time, we couldn't have imagined anything stronger. But it is, and it's everywhere. People are pressing pills out of this stuff to look like other pills. Kids are dying. Kids fifteen and sixteen years old, just like us, experimenting. But they don't have that luxury anymore because the pills they are sold might not be what they thought they bought. And one pill kills them. I know we wouldn't have survived our teen years in this day and age. Now I have to think about raising a kid in all of this. Knowing he is genetically predisposed to addiction and that there isn't any room for mistakes with today's drugs. But you know how it is trying to tell a kid that.

Hell, we knew that. We knew we were playing with fire when we took that first drink. I don't know if you worried about becoming addicted, but I always thought I was smarter than that and had more self-control—like somehow, I could defy nature. Tripp is ten, so it's getting about that time. He already tells me I'm overprotective and worry too much. But he doesn't understand the things I've seen. I've never told him I'm in recovery. That conversation will come soon enough, I guess. But I will be overprotective. And I'll ask him about his feelings and who he's running around with. And I won't let him drink at my house because it's safer than being on the road. Because I think that's a bunch of shit now. Anybody who ever told us that should have wanted more for us. It was their job to protect us. Hopefully, I've shown him what a good time without alcohol and drugs looks like, so he doesn't think he has to have it, like we did.

A lot of people I run around with now don't know the old me. Hell, some people have even questioned if I'm really an addict. I have to defend my recovery all the time. Can you believe that? With all the shit we did. People still don't understand addiction, and it's frustrating. I wish you were here. Maybe you could have gotten clean. It's pretty amazing what happens when you get in recovery. I would have loved that for you.

But it wasn't in the cards. For whatever reason, you were taken away too soon. And the only memory of you that Tripp will ever have is from a faded photo when he was four months old. His mind won't whirl with memories whenever he hears Pink Floyd or watches *Wayne's World*. Right now, he doesn't know you at all. He knows I have a cousin who died. But he doesn't really know you, because I keep you with me and on the page. I don't think anybody wants to hear about it anymore. Grief makes people uncomfortable. They don't know what to say or how to react to someone in pain. And that's okay. I don't expect them to. It's mine to carry. But sometimes, there are nods from you that come through to this world, and it makes me wonder about what's beyond.

I thought about you on a recent trip to Red River Gorge, where I took Tripp away for a couple of days during spring break. We rented a cabin. He thinks there is nothing better than a cabin in the Gorge. We hiked and ate good pizza. Spent the evening in the hot tub, counting the stars. I can talk to him here, out of his routine and environment, and sometimes he will let me in on what he's thinking. Out of the blue, he says, "Mommy, spell 'I cup.'" It stopped me in my tracks. I tried not to look alarmed, but there you were. Ten years old, bugging us all with your new joke. Shannon got so annoyed that she would say, "We know, Eric, I see you pee in my backyard." Somehow the "in my backyard" part was added, which has nothing to do with the joke. I looked at him and saw he was excited, ready to get one over on me. I let him. I went along with it, spelling out "I cup" as if I had never heard it before.

Moments like these make me wonder. Does that joke live in the walls of a fifth-grade classroom, waiting for kids of all generations? Or do our loved ones speak to us in ways only we can understand? This was the joke that you could have told him. The memory he could have had with you. Maybe somehow you did. Somehow you got through. But he won't know it was you. Only I do. And that's why I keep you close and only on the page.

MANDI

Mandi and Eric, Headstart Graduation

Acknowledgments

First and foremost, I want to thank Abby Freeland, Ashley Runyon, and the University Press of Kentucky for giving my words, and the words of so many underrepresented voices in Appalachia, a place to land. To Gurney Norman, who helped me understand the importance of place and voice. To my husband, PJ, for his patience and understanding. To my son, Tripp, whose love and laughter have been a constant source of joy and inspiration. I am proud to be his mother. To Meredith McCarroll for her tender encouragement, insightful feedback, and unwavering support throughout the process. When I wasn't sure I could go on, she was there to remind me that this work is important and worthy. To the community of writers who convene every summer at the Hindman Settlement School for the Appalachian Writers' Workshop, whose names are too numerous to list. My confidence and courage came here in workshops, on porches, and over meals. I found a home when I found my community. To Robert Gipe for his generous spirit and badass map-making skills. Bless you, Robert, for reading all the drafts! Love you, buddy. To Melissa Helton for her gentle nudge to put words on the page every day. To Annette Saunooke Clapsaddle, who was there, day in and day out, to celebrate the victories and the setbacks. Your belief in me and willingness to listen have been invaluable. All the Jason Isbell concerts didn't hurt, either. I consider myself lucky to call you my friend. Thank you to all who have supported me on this journey. Your kindness and generosity have meant more to me than words can express. To all of you out there living "Just for Today."

About the Author

Mandi Fugate Sheffel was born and raised in Red Fox, Kentucky. She is a graduate of Eastern Kentucky University and is currently the Sycamore Fund project coordinator at the Foundation for Appalachian Kentucky. She is the board vice chair of the Appalachian Arts Alliance and a Mountain Association board member. Additionally, she owns and operates Read Spotted Newt, an independent bookstore in the coalfields of eastern Kentucky. She found her passion for writing and storytelling at the Appalachian Writers' Workshop at the Hindman Settlement School. Her personal essays and opinion pieces can be found in *Still: The Journal*, *Lexington Herald-Leader*, and the *Courier Journal*.